The Chaldean Account of Genesis

THE CHALDEAN ACCOUNT

OF GENESIS.

IZDUBAR (NIMROD) IN CONFLICT WITH A LION.

FROM AN EARLY BABYLONIAN CYLINDER.

IS.

ON,

THE

CHALDEAN ACCOUNT OF GENESIS.

CONTAINING

THE DESCRIPTION OF THE CREATION, THE FALL OF MAN,

THE DELUGE, THE TOWER OF BABEL, THE

TIMES OF THE PATRIARCHS,

AND NIMROD;

BABYLONIAN FABLES, AND LEGENDS OF THE GODS;

FROM THE CUNEIFORM INSCRIPTIONS.

BY GEORGE SMITH,

OF THE DEPARTMENT OF ORIENTAL ANTIQUITIES, BRITISH MUSEUM,

AUTHOR OF " HISTORY OF ASSURBANIPAL,"

"ASSYRIAN DISCOVERIES,"

ETC. ETC.

WITH ILLUSTRATIONS.

Fourth Edition.

LONDON:

SAMPSON LOW, MARSTON, SEARLE, AND RIVINGTON,

CROWN BUILDINGS, FLEET STREET.

1876.

TO

SIR HENRY CRESWICKE RAWLINSON,

K.C.B., D.C.L., ETC. ETC. ETC.,

MY TEACHER AND PREDECESSOR IN MY PRESENT

LINE OF RESEARCH,

IN REMEMBRANCE OF MANY FAVOURS,

THIS WORK IS

Dedicated.

INTRODUCTION.

SOME explanation is necessary in introducing my present work. Little time has elapsed since I discovered the most important of these inscriptions, and in the intervening period I have had, amidst other work, to collect the various fragments of the legends, copy, compare, and translate, altering my matter from time to time, as new fragments turned up. Even now I have gone to press with one of the fragments of the last tablet of the Izdubar series omitted.

The present condition of the legends and their recent discovery alike forbid me to call this anything more than a provisional work; but there was so general a desire to see the translations that I have published them, hoping my readers will take them with the same reserve with which I have given them.

I have avoided some of the most important comparisons and conclusions with respect to Genesis, as my desire was first to obtain the recognition of the evidence without prejudice.

The chronological notes in the book are one of its weak points, but I may safely say that I have placed the various dates as low as I fairly could, considering the evidence, and I have aimed to do this rather than to establish any system of chronology.

I believe that time will show the Babylonian traditions of Genesis to be invaluable for the light they will throw on the Pentateuch, but at present there are so many blanks in the evidence that positive conclusions on several points are impossible. I may add in conclusion that my present work is intended as a popular account, and I have introduced only so much explanation as seems necessary for the proper understanding of the subject. I have added translations of some parts of the legends which I avoided in my last work, desiring here to satisfy the wish to see them as perfect as possible; there still remain however some passages which I have omitted, but these are of small extent and obscure.

October 26, 1875.

CONTENTS.

CHAPTER I.—THE DISCOVERY OF THE GENESIS LEGENDS.

Cosmogony of Berosus.—Discovery of Cuneiform Inscriptions.—Historical Texts.—Babylonian origin of Assyrian literature.—Mythological tablets. —Discovery of Deluge texts.—Izdubar, his exploits.—Mutilated condition of tablets.—Lecture on Deluge tablets.—"Daily Telegraph" offer.—Expedition to Assyria.—Fragments of Creation tablets.—Solar Myth.—Second journey to Assyria.—Tower of Babel.—Clay records.—Account of creation in "Telegraph."— "Daily Telegraph" collection.—Interest of Creation legends.—The Fall.—New fragments.—List of texts . . . page 1

CHAPTER II.—BABYLONIAN AND ASSYRIAN LITERATURE.

Babylonian literature.—Kouyunjik library.—Fragmentary condition.—Arrangement of tablets.—Subjects.—Dates.—Babylonian source of literature.—Literary period.—Babylonian Chronology.— Akkad.—Sumir.—Urukh, king of Ur.—Hammurabi.—Babylonian astrology.—War of Gods.—Izdubar legends.—Creation and fall.— Syllabaries and bilingual tablets.—Assyrian copies.—Difficulties as to date.—Mutilated condition.—Babylonian library.—Assyrian empire.—City of Assur.—Library at Calah.—Sargon of Assyria.— Sennacherib.—Removal of Library to Nineveh.—Assurbanipal or Sardanapalus.—His additions to library.—Description of contents. —Later Babylonian libraries 19

CHAPTER III.—CHALDEAN LEGENDS TRANSMITTED THROUGH BEROSUS AND OTHER ANCIENT AUTHORS.

Berosus and his copyists.—Cory's translation.—Alexander Polyhistor.—Babylonia.—Oannes, his teaching.—Creation.—Belus.—Chaldean kings.—Xisuthrus.—Deluge.—The Ark.—Return to Babylon.—Apollodorus.—Pantibiblon.—Larancha.—Abydenus.—Alorus, first king.—Ten kings.—Sisithrus.—Deluge.—Armenia.—Tower of Babel.—Cronos and Titan.—Nicolaus Damascenus.—Dispersion from Hestiæus.—Babylonian colonies.—Tower of Babel.—The Sibyl.—Titan and Prometheus.—Damascius.—Tauthe.—Moymis.—Kissare and Assorus.—Triad.—Bel . . . 37

CHAPTER IV.—BABYLONIAN MYTHOLOGY.

Greek accounts.—Mythology local in origin.—Antiquity.—Conquests.—Colonies.—Three great gods.—Twelve great gods.—Angels.—Spirits.—Anu.—Anatu.—Vul.—Ishtar.—Equivalent to Venus.—Hea.—Oannes.—Merodach.—Bel or Jupiter.—Ziratbanit, Succoth Benoth.—Elu.—Sin the moon god.—Ninip.—Shamas.—Nergal.—Anunit.—Table of gods 51

CHAPTER V.—BABYLONIAN LEGEND OF THE CREATION.

Mutilated condition of tablets.—List of subjects.—Description of chaos.—Tiamat.—Generation of gods.—Damascius.—Comparison with Genesis.—Three great gods.—Doubtful fragments.—Fifth tablet.—Stars.—Planets.—Moon.—Sun.—Abyss or chaos.—Creation of moon.—Creation of animals.—Man.—His duties.—Dragon of sea.—Fall.—Curse for disobedience.—Discussion.—Sacred tree.—Dragon or serpent.—War with Tiamat.—Weapons.—Merodach.—Destruction of Tiamat.—Mutilation of documents.—Parallel Biblical account.—Age of story 61

CHAPTER VI.—OTHER BABYLONIAN ACCOUNTS OF THE CREATION.

Cuneiform accounts originally traditions.—Variations.—Account of Berosus.—Tablet from Cutha.—Translation.—Composite animals.—Eagle-headed men.—Seven brothers.—Destruction of men.—Seven wicked spirits.—War in heaven.—Variations of story.—Poetical account of Creation 101

CHAPTER VII.—THE SIN OF THE GOD ZU.

God Zu.—Obscurity of legend.—Translation.—Sin of Zu.—

Anger of the gods.—Speeches of Anu to Vul.—Vul's answer.—
Speech of Anu to Nebo.—Answer of Nebo.—Sarturda.—Changes
to a bird.—The Zu bird.—Bird of prey.—Sarturda lord of
Amarda 113

CHAPTER VIII.—THE EXPLOITS OF LUBARA.
Lubara.—God of Pestilence.—Itak.—The Plague.—Seven
warrior gods.—Destruction of people.—Anu.—Goddess of Karrak.
—Speech of Elu.—Sin and destruction of Babylonians.—Shamas.—
Sin and destruction of Erech.—Ishtar.—The great god and
Duran.—Cutha.—Internal wars.—Itak goes to Syria.—Power
and glory of Lubara.—Song of Lubara.—Blessings on his worship.
—God Ner.—Prayer to arrest the Plague . . . 123

CHAPTER IX.—BABYLONIAN FABLES.
Fables.—Common in the East.—Description.—Power of speech
in animals.—Story of the eagle.—Serpent.—Shamas.—The eagle
caught.—Eats the serpent.—Anger of birds.—Etana.—Seven
gods.—Third tablet.—Speech of eagle.—Story of the fox.—His
cunning.—Judgment of Shamas.—His show of sorrow.—His
punishment.—Speech of fox.—Fable of the horse and ox.—They
consort together.—Speech of the ox.—His good fortune.—Con-
trast with the horse.—Hunting the ox.—Speech of the horse.—
Offers to recount story.—Story of Ishtar.—Further tablets . 137

CHAPTER X.—FRAGMENTS OF MISCELLANEOUS TEXTS.
Atarpi.—Sin of the world.—Mother and daughter quarrel.—Zamu.
—Punishment of world.—Hea.—Calls his sons.—Orders drought.
—Famine.—Building.—Nusku.—Riddle of wise man.—Nature
and universal presence of air.—Gods.—Sinuri.—Divining by frac-
ture of reed.—Incantation.—Dream.—Tower of Babel.—Obscurity
of legend.—Not noticed by Berosus.—Fragmentary tablet.—Destruction of Tower.—Dispersion.—Locality of Babylon.—Birs Nimrud.—Babil.—Assyrian representations 153

CHAPTER XI.—THE IZDUBAR LEGENDS.
Account of Deluge.—Nimrod.—Izdubar.—Age of Legends.—
Babylonian cylinders.—Notices of Izdubar.—Surippak.—Ark City.

—Twelve tablets.—Extent of Legends.—Description.—Introduction.—Meeting of Heabani and Izdubar.—Destruction of tyrant Humbaba.—Adventures of Ishtar.—Illness and wanderings of Izdubar.—Description of Deluge and conclusion.—First Tablet.—Kingdom of Nimrod.—Traditions.—Identifications.—Translation.—Elamite Conquest.—Dates 167

CHAPTER XII.—MEETING OF HEABANI AND IZDUBAR.
Dream of Izdubar.—Heabani.—His wisdom.—His solitary life.—Izdubar's petition.—Zaidu.—Harimtu and Samhat.—Tempt Heabani.—Might and fame of Izdubar.—Speech of Heabani.—His journey to Erech.—The midannu or tiger.—Festival at Erech.—Dream of Izdubar.—Friendship with Heabani .   . 193

CHAPTER XIII.—DESTRUCTION OF THE TYRANT HUMBABA.
Elamite dominion.—Forest region.—Humbaba.—Conversation.—Petition to Shamas.—Journey to forest.—Dwelling of Humbaba.—Entrance to forest.—Meeting with Humbaba.—Death of Humbaba.—Izdubar king 207

CHAPTER XIV.—THE ADVENTURES OF ISHTAR.
Triumph of Izdubar.—Ishtar's love.—Her offer of marriage.—Her promises.—Izdubar's answer.—Tammuz.—Amours of Ishtar.—His refusal.—Ishtar's anger.—Ascends to Heaven.—The bull.—Slain by Izdubar.—Ishtar's curse.—Izdubar's triumph.—The feast.—Ishtar's despair.—Her descent to Hades.—Description.—The seven gates.—The curses.—Uddusunamir.—Sphinx.—Release of Ishtar.—Lament for Tammuz 217

CHAPTER XV.—ILLNESS AND WANDERINGS OF IZDUBAR.
Heabani and the trees.—Illness of Izdubar.—Death of Heabani.—Journey of Izdubar.—His dream.—Scorpion men.—The Desert of Mas.—The paradise.—Siduri and Sabitu.—Urhamsi.—Water of death.—Ragmu.—The conversation.—Hasisadra 241

CHAPTER XVI.—THE STORY OF THE FLOOD AND CONCLUSION.
Eleventh tablet.—The gods.—Sin of the world.—Command to build the ark.—Its contents.—The building.—The Flood.—Destruction of people.—Fear of the gods.—End of Deluge.—Nizir.—

Resting of Ark.—The birds.—The descent from the ark.—The sacrifice.—Speeches of gods.—Translation of Hasisadra.—Cure of Izdubar.—His return.—Lament over Heabani.—Resurrection of Heabani.—Burial of warrior.—Comparison with Genesis.—Syrian nation.—Connection of legends.—Points of contact.—Duration of deluge.—Mount of descent.—Ten generations.—Early cities.— Age of Izdubar 263

CHAPTER XVII.—CONCLUSION.
    Notices of Genesis.—Correspondence of names.—Abram.—Ur of Chaldees.—Ishmael.—Sargon.—His birth.—Concealed in ark. —Age of Nimrod.—Doubtful theories.—Creation.—Garden of Eden.—Oannes.—Berosus.—Izdubar legends.—Urukh of Ur.— Babylonian seals.—Egyptian names.—Assyrian sculptures . 295

LIST OF ILLUSTRATIONS.

FRONTISPIECE, Photograph. Izdubar (Nimrod) in conflict with a lion, from an early Babylonian cylinder.

2. Reverse of inscribed terra cotta tablet, containing the account of the Deluge, showing the various fragments of which it is composed, 10.

3. Oannes and other Babylonian mythological figures, from cylinder, 39.

4. Composite animals, from cylinder, 41.

5. Fight between Merodach (Bel) and the dragon, to face p. 62.

6. Sacred tree or grove, with attendant cherubim, from Assyrian cylinder, 89.

7. Sacred tree, seated figure on each side and serpent in background, from an early Babylonian cylinder, 91.

8. Bel encountering the dragon, from Babylonian cylinder, 95.

9. Merodach or Bel armed for the conflict with the dragon, from Assyrian cylinder, 99.

10. Fight between Bel and the dragon, from Babylonian cylinder, 102.

11. Eagle-headed men, from Nimroud sculpture, to face p. 102.

12. Sacred tree, attendant figures and eagle-headed men, from the seal of a Syrian chief, ninth century B.C., 106.

13. Men engaged in building, from Babylonian cylinder, 158.

14 and 15. Men engaged in building, from Babylonian cylinders, 159.

16. View of Birs Nimrud, the supposed site of the Tower of Babel, 162.

17. View of the Babil mound at Babylon, the site of the temple of Bel, 163.

18. Tower in stages, from an Assyrian bas-relief, 164.

19. Izdubar strangling a lion, from Khorsabad sculpture, to face p. 174.

20. Migration of Eastern tribe, from early Babylonian cylinder, 188.

21. Bowareyeh Mound at Warka (Erech), site of the temple of Ishtar, 237.

22. Izdubar and Heabani in conflict with the lion and bull, 239.

23. Izdubar, composite figures, and Hasisadra (Noah) in the ark, from early Babylonian cylinder, 257.

24. Composite figures (scorpion men), from an Assyrian cylinder, 262.

25. Hasisadra, or Noah, and Izdubar, from an early Babylonian cylinder, 283.

26. Mugheir, the site of Ur of the Chaldees, 297.

27. Oannes, from Nimroud sculpture, to face p. 306.

Chapter I.

THE DISCOVERY OF THE GENESIS LEGENDS.

Cosmogony of Berosus.—Discovery of Cuneiform Inscriptions.
—Historical texts.—Babylonian origin of Assyrian literature.—
Mythological tablets.—Discovery of Deluge texts.—Izdubar, his
exploits.—Mutilated condition of tablets.—Lecture on Deluge
tablets.—" Daily Telegraph " offer.—Expedition to Assyria.—
Fragments of Creation tablets.—Solar Myth.—Second journey to
Assyria.—Tower of Babel.—Clay records.—Account of creation
in " Telegraph."—" Daily Telegraph " collection.—Interest of
Creation legends.—The Fall.—New fragments.—List of texts.

THE fragments of the Chaldean historian,
Berosus, preserved in the works of
various later writers, have shown that
the Babylonians were acquainted with
traditions referring to the Creation, the period before
the Flood, the Deluge, and other matters forming
parts of Genesis.

Berosus, however, who recorded these events,
lived in the time of Alexander the Great and his
successors, somewhere about B.C. 330 to 260; and, as
this was three hundred years after the Jews were
carried captive to Babylon, his works did not prove

B

that these traditions were in Babylonia before the Jewish captivity, and could not afford testimony in favour of the great antiquity of these legends.

On the discovery and decipherment of the cuneiform inscriptions, Oriental scholars hoped that copies of the Babylonian histories and traditions would one day be discovered, and we should thus gain earlier and more satisfactory evidence as to these primitive histories.

In the mound of Kouyunjik, opposite the town of Mosul, Mr. Layard discovered part of the Royal Assyrian library, and further collections, also forming parts of this library, have been subsequently found by Mr. H. Rassam, Mr. Loftus, and myself. Sir Henry Rawlinson, who made the preliminary examination of Mr. Layard's treasures, and who was the first to recognize their value, estimated the number of these fragments of inscriptions at over twenty thousand.

The attention of decipherers was in the first instance drawn to the later historical inscriptions, particularly to those of the Assyrian kings contemporary with the Hebrew monarchy; and in this section of inscriptions a very large number of texts of great importance rewarded the toil of Assyrian scholars. Inscriptions of Tiglath Pileser, Shalmaneser, Sargon, Sennacherib, Esarhaddon, Nebuchadnezzar, Nabonidus, and numerous other ancient sovereigns, bearing directly on the Bible, and giving new light upon parts of ancient history before obscure, for a long time occupied almost exclusively the attention of students, and overshadowed any work in other divisions of Assyrian literature.

Although it was known that Assyria borrowed its civilization and written characters from Babylonia, yet, as the Assyrian nation was mostly hostile to the southern and older kingdom, it could not be guessed beforehand that the peculiar national traditions of Babylonia would be transported to Assyria.

Under these circumstances, for some years after the cuneiform inscriptions were first deciphered, nothing was looked for or discovered bearing upon the events of Genesis; but, as new texts were brought into notice, it became evident that the Assyrians copied their literature largely from Babylonian sources, and it appeared likely that search among the fragments of Assyrian inscriptions would yield traces at least of some of these ancient Babylonian legends.

Attention was early drawn to these points by Sir Henry Rawlinson, who pointed out several coincidences between the geography of Babylonia and the account of Eden in Genesis, and suggested the great probability that the accounts in Genesis had a Babylonian origin.

When at work preparing the fourth volume of Cuneiform Inscriptions, I noticed references to the Creation in a tablet numbered K 63 in the Museum collection, and allusions in other tablets to similar legends; I therefore set about searching through the collection, which I had previously selected under the head of " Mythological tablets," to find, if possible, some of these legends.　This mythological collection was one of six divisions into which I had parted the Museum collection of cuneiform inscriptions for convenience of working.　By placing all the tablets and fragments of the same class together, I had been able to complete several texts, to easily find any subject required, and at any time to get a general idea of the contents of the collection.

The mythological division contained all tablets relating to the mythology, and all the legends in which the gods took a leading part, together with prayers and similar subjects.

Commencing a steady search among these fragments, I soon found half of a curious tablet which had evidently contained originally six columns of text; two of these (the third and fourth) were still nearly perfect; two others (the second and fifth) were imperfect, about half remaining, while the remaining columns (the first and sixth) were entirely lost.　On looking down the third column, my eye caught the statement that the ship rested on the mountains of Nizir, followed by the account of the sending forth of the dove, and its finding no resting-place and returning.　I saw at once that I had here discovered a portion at least of the Chaldean account of the Deluge.　I then proceeded to read through the document, and found it was in the form of a speech from the hero of the Deluge to a person

whose name appeared to be Izdubar. I recollected
a legend belonging to the same hero Izdubar K. 231,
which, on comparison, proved to belong to the same
series, and then I commenced a search for any missing portions of the tablets.

This search was a long and heavy work, for there
were thousands of fragments to go over, and, while
on the one side I had gained as yet only two fragments of the Izdubar legends to judge from, on the
other hand, the unsorted fragments were so small,
and contained so little of the subject, that it was
extremely difficult to ascertain their meaning. My
search, however, proved successful. I found a fragment of another copy of the Deluge, containing again
the sending forth of the birds, and gradually collected several other portions of this tablet, fitting
them in one after another until I had completed the
greater part of the second column. Portions of a
third copy next turned up, which, when joined
together, completed a considerable part of the first
and sixth columns. I now had the account of the
Deluge in the state in which I published it at the
meeting of the Society of Biblical Archæology,
December 3rd, 1872. I had discovered that the
Izdubar series contained at least twelve tablets, and
I afterwards found this to be their exact number.
Of this series the tablet describing the Deluge was
the eleventh and K 231. the sixth. Numerous other
fragments turned up at the same time; but these,
while they increased my knowledge of the legends,

could not be arranged in order from want of indication of the particular tablets to which they belonged.

Some other fragmentary legends, including the war of the gods and three fables, I also found at the same time, but these were in such mutilated condition that I could not make a connected translation of them.

In my lecture on the Deluge tablets, I gave a sketch of the Izdubar legends, and expressed my belief that the Chaldean inscriptions contained various other similar stories bearing upon the Book of Genesis, which would prove of the highest interest.

Just at this time happened the intervention of the proprietors of the "Daily Telegraph" newspaper. Mr. E. Arnold, who is on the direction of that paper, had already sent to me expressing his interest in these discoveries, and immediately after my lecture he came armed with a proposition from the proprietors of the "Daily Telegraph" to re-open, at their cost, the excavations in Assyria, and gain some new information on the subject of these legends. This proposition was submitted to the trustees of the British Museum, and they directed me to go to Assyria and make a short excavation, leave of absence for six months being granted to me for this purpose. I have related, in my work, "Assyrian discoveries," the history of this expedition, which brought me the next fragments of these legends. Soon after I commenced excavating at Kouyunjik, on the site of the palace of Assurbanipal, I found a

new fragment of the Chaldean account of the Deluge
belonging to the first column of the tablet, relating
the command to build and fill the ark, and nearly
filling up the most considerable blank in the story.
Some other fragments, which I found afterwards,
still further completed this tablet, which was already
the most perfect one in the Izdubar series. The
trench in which I found the fragment in question
must have passed very near the place where the
Assyrians kept a series of inscriptions belonging
to the early history of the world. Soon after I
discovered the fragment of the Deluge tablet, I
came upon a fragment of the sixth tablet of the
same series in this trench, and not far from the place
of the Deluge fragment. This fragment described
the destruction of the bull of Ishtar by Izdubar and
Heabani, an incident often depicted on early Babylonian gems. My next discovery here was a fragment evidently belonging to the creation of the
world; this was the upper corner of a tablet, and
gave a fragmentary account of the creation of
animals. Further on in this trench I discovered
two other portions of this legend, one giving the
Creation and fall of man; the other having part of
the war between the gods and evil spirits. At that
time I did not recognize the importance of these
fragments, excepting the one with the account of the
creation of animals, and, as I had immediately afterwards to return to England, I made no further discoveries in this direction.

On my return from the east, I published some of
the discoveries I had made, and I now found, on
joining the fragments of the Deluge or Izdubar series,
that they formed exactly twelve tablets. The fact
that these legends covered twelve tablets led to the
impression that they were a form of the solar myth,
that is, that they symbolized the passage of the sun
through the heavens, each tablet representing a
separate sign of the zodiac. This opinion, first
started by Sir Henry Rawlinson, was at once accepted by M. Lenormant, Rev. A. H. Sayce, and
other scholars; but I think myself it rests on too
insecure a basis to be true. In a subsequent chapter
I will give as nearly as I can the contents of the
Izdubar legends, which I think do not warrant this
view. Some months further passed, during which
I was engaged in my second journey to Assyria, and
in realizing the results of that expedition. I again
brought from Assyria several fragments of the
Genesis legends which helped to complete these
curious stories, and in January, 1875, I commenced
once more a regular search for these fragments.
Very soon afterwards I succeeded in discovering a
notice of the building of the tower of Babel, which
at once attracted attention, and a notice of it, which
appeared in the " Athenæum," No. 2468, was copied
into several of the papers. I was, however, at that
time hardly prepared to publish these legends, as I
had not ascertained how far they could be completed
from our present collections.

Subsequent search did not show that any further fragments of the Babel tablet were in the British Museum, but I soon added several fresh portions to the fragmentary history of the Creation and Fall. The greatest difficulty with which I had to contend in all these researches was the extremely mutilated and deficient condition in which the tablets were found. There can be no doubt that, if the inscriptions were perfect, they would present very little difficulty to the translator.

The reason why these legends are in so many fragments, and the different parts so scattered, may be explained from the nature of the material of which the tablets are composed, and the changes undergone by them since they were written. These tablets were composed of fine clay and were inscribed with cuneiform characters while in a soft state; they were then baked in a furnace until hard, and afterwards transferred to the library. These texts appear to have been broken up when Nineveh was destroyed, and many of them were cracked and scorched by the heat at the burning of the palace. Subsequently the ruins were turned over in search of treasure, and the tablets still further broken; and then, to complete their ruin, the rain, every spring soaking through the ground, saturates them with water containing chemicals, and these chemicals form crystals in every available crack. The growth of the crystals further splits the tablets, some of them being literally shivered.

Some idea of the mutilated condition of the Assyrian tablets, and of the work of restoring a single text, will be gained from the engraving below, which exhibits the present appearance of one of the Deluge tablets.   In this tablet there are sixteen fragments.

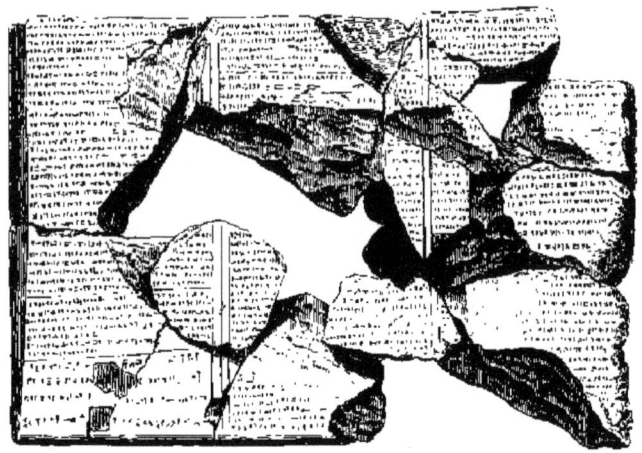

REVERSE OF INSCRIBED TERRA COTTA TABLET CONTAINING THE ACCOUNT
OF THE DELUGE, SHOWING THE VARIOUS FRAGMENTS OF WHICH IT
IS COMPOSED.

The clay records of the Assyrians are by these means so broken up, that they are in some cases divided into over one hundred fragments; and it is only by collecting and joining together the various fragments that these ancient texts can be restored. Many of the old fragmentary tablets which have been twenty years in the British Museum have been added to considerably by fragments which I found during my two journeys, and yet there remain at least 20,000 fragments buried in the ruins without the recovery of which it is impossible to complete these valuable Assyrian inscriptions.

Being now urged by many friends who were interested in the subject, I sent the following account to the editor of the " Daily Telegraph," which was printed in that paper on the 4th of March, 1875 :—

" Having recently made a series of important discoveries relating to the Book of Genesis, among some remarkable texts, which form part of the collection presented to the British Museum by the proprietors of ' The Daily Telegraph,' I venture once more to bring Assyrian subjects before your readers.

" In my lecture on the Chaldean Account of the Deluge, which I delivered on Dec. 3, 1872, I stated my conviction that all the earlier narratives of Genesis would receive new light from the inscriptions so long buried in the Chaldean and Assyrian mounds; but I little thought at that time that I was so near to finding most of them.

" My lecture, as your readers know, was soon followed by the proposal of your proprietors and the organizing of ' The Daily Telegraph ' expedition to Assyria. When excavating at Kouyunjik during that expedition, I discovered the missing portion of the first column of the Deluge tablet, an account of which I sent home; and in the same trench I subsequently found the fragment which I afterwards recognized as part of the Chaldean story of the

Creation, which relic I have noticed already in your
columns. I excavated later on, while still working
under your auspices, another portion belonging to
this story, far more precious—in fact, I think, to the
general public, the most interesting and remarkable
cuneiform tablet yet discovered. This turns out to
contain the story of man's original innocence, of the
temptation, and of the fall. I was, when I found it,
on the eve of departing, and had not time to properly
examine my great prize. I only copied the two or
three first lines, which (as I had then no idea of the
general subject of the tablet) did not appear very
valuable, and I forthwith packed it in the box for
transport to England, where it arrived safely, and
was presented by the proprietors of 'The Daily
Telegraph,' with the rest of their collection, to the
British Museum. On my return to England I made
some other discoveries among my store, and in the
pursuit of these this fragment was overlooked. I
subsequently went a second time to Assyria, and returned to England in June, 1874 ; but I had no
leisure to look again at those particular legends until
the end of January in this year. Then, starting
with the fragment of the Creation in 'The Daily
Telegraph' collection, which I had first noticed, I
began to collect other portions of the series, and
among these I soon found the overlooked fragment
which I had excavated at Kouyunjik, the first lines
of which I took down in the note-book of my first
expedition. I subsequently found several smaller

pieces in the old Museum collection, and all join or form parts of a continuous series of legends, giving the history of the world from the Creation down to some period after the Fall of Man. Linked with these, I found also other series of legends on primitive history, including the story of the building of the Tower of Babel and of the Confusion of Tongues.

" The first series, which I may call ' The Story of the Creation and Fall,' when complete must have consisted of nine or ten tablets at least, and the history upon it is much longer and fuller than the corresponding account in the Book of Genesis. With respect to these Genesis narratives a furious strife has existed for many years; every word has been scanned by eager scholars, and every possible meaning which the various passages could bear has been suggested; while the age and authenticity of the narratives have been discussed on all sides. In particular, it may be said that the account of the fall of man, the heritage of all Christian countries, has been the centre of this controversy, for it is one of the pivots on which the Christian religion turns. The world-wide importance of these subjects will therefore give the newly discovered inscriptions, and especially the one relating to the Fall, an unparalleled value, and I am glad, indeed, that such a treasure should have resulted from your expedition.

" Whatever the primitive account may have been

from which the earlier part of the Book of Genesis was copied, it is evident that the brief narration given in the Pentateuch omits a number of incidents and explanations—for instance, as to the origin of evil, the fall of the angels, the wickedness of the serpent, &c. Such points as these are included in the Cuneiform narrative; but of course I can say little about them until I prepare full translations of the legends.

"The narrative on the Assyrian tablets commences with a description of the period before the world was created, when there existed a chaos or confusion. The desolate and empty state of the universe and the generation by chaos of monsters are vividly given. The chaos is presided over by a female power named Tisalat and Tiamat, corresponding to the Thalatth of Berosus; but, as it proceeds, the Assyrian account agrees rather with the Bible than with the short account from Berosus. We are told, in the inscriptions, of the fall of the celestial being who appears to correspond to Satan. In his ambition he raises his hand against the sanctuary of the God of heaven, and the description of him is really magnificent. He is represented riding in a chariot through celestial space, surrounded by the storms, with the lightning playing before him, and wielding a thunderbolt as a weapon.

"This rebellion leads to a war in heaven and the conquest of the powers of evil, the gods in due course creating the universe in stages, as in the

Mosaic narrative, surveying each step of the work and pronouncing it good. The divine work culminates in the creation of man, who is made upright and free from evil, and endowed by the gods with the noble faculty of speech.

" The Deity then delivers a long address to the newly created being, instructing him in all his duties and privileges, and pointing out the glory of his state. But this condition of blessing does not last long before man, yielding to temptation, falls; and the Deity then pronounces upon him a terrible curse, invoking on his head all the evils which have since afflicted humanity. These last details are, as I have before stated, upon the fragment which I excavated during my first journey to Assyria, and the discovery of this single relic in my opinion increases many times over the value of ' The Daily Telegraph ' collection.

" I have at present recovered no more of the story, and am not yet in a position to give the full translations and details; but I hope during the spring to find time to search over the collection of smaller fragments of tablets, and to light upon any smaller parts of the legends which may have escaped me. There will arise, besides, a number of important questions as to the date and origin of the legends, their comparison with the Biblical narrative, and as to how far they may supplement the Mosaic account."

This will serve to exhibit the appearance these

legends presented to me soon after I discovered them.

On comparing this account with the translations and notes I have given in this book, it will be evident that my first notice was inaccurate in several points, both as to the order and translation of the legends; but I had not expected it to be otherwise, for there had not been time to collect and translate the fragments, and, until that was done, no satisfactory account of them could be given, the inaccuracies in the account being due to the broken state of the tablets and my recent knowledge of them. It is a notable fact that the discovery of these legends was one of the fruits of the expedition organized by the proprietors of the "Daily Telegraph," and these legends and the Deluge fragments form the most valuable results of that expedition.

After I had published this notice in the "Daily Telegraph" I set to work to look over the fragments in the collection, in search of other minor fragments, and found several, but these added little to my knowledge, only enabling me to correct my notice. A little later I discovered a new fragment of the tenth tablet of the Deluge series, and last of all a further portion of the sixth tablet of these legends. This closed my discoveries so far as the fragments of the tablets were concerned, and I had then to copy and translate the tablets as far as their mutilated condition would allow.

The Genesis legends which I had collected from

the various Assyrian fragments included numerous other stories beside those which parallel the account in the Book of Genesis. All these stories are similar in character, and appear to belong to the same early literary age. So far as I have made out they are as follows :—

1. A long account of the origin of the world, the creation of the animals and man, the fall of man from a sinless state, and a conflict between the gods and the powers of evil.

2. A second account of the creation having a closer correspondence with the account of Berosus.

3. A Bilingual legend of the history of the seven evil spirits, apparently part of a third version of the creation.

4. Story of the descent of the goddess Ishtar or Venus into Hades, and her return.

5. Legend of the sin of the God Zu, who insults Elu, the father of the gods.

6. Collection of five tablets giving the exploits of Lubara the god of the pestilence.

7. Legend of the god Sarturda, who turned into a bird.

8. Story of the wise man who put forth a riddle to the gods.

9. Legend of the good man Atarpi, and the wickedness of the world.

10. Legend of the tower of Babel, and dispersion.

11. Story of the Eagle and Etana.

12. Story of the ox and the horse.

13. Story of the fox.

14. Legend of Sinuri.

15. Izdubar legends: twelve tablets, with the history of Izdubar, and an account of the flood.

16. Various fragments of other legends. These show that there was a considerable collection of such primitive stories almost unrepresented in our present collection.

CHAPTER II.

BABYLONIAN AND ASSYRIAN LITERATURE.

Babylonian literature.—Kouyunjik library.—Fragmentary condition.—Arrangement of tablets.—Subjects.—Dates.—Babylonian source of literature.—Literary period.—Babylonian Chronology.—Akkad.—Sumir.—Urukh, king of Ur.—Hammurabi.—Babylonian astrology. — War of Gods. — Izdubar legends.—Creation and fall.—Syllabaries and bilingual tablets.—Assyrian copies.—Difficulties as to date.—Mutilated condition.—Babylonian library.—Assyrian empire.—City of Assur.—Library at Calah.—Sargon of Assyria.—Sennacherib.—Removal of Library to Nineveh.—Assurbanipal or Sardanapalus.—His additions to library.—Description of contents.—Later Babylonian libraries.

N order to understand the position of these legends it is necessary to give some account of the wonderful literature of the Ancient Babylonians and their copyists, the Assyrians. The fragments of terra cotta tablets containing these legends were found in the débris which covers the palaces called the South West Palace and the North Palace at Kouyunjik; the former building being of the age of Sennacherib, the latter belonging to the time of Assurbanipal. The tablets, which are of all sizes, from one inch long to over a foot square, are nearly all in fragments, and

in consequence of the changes which have taken place in the ruins the fragments of the same tablet are sometimes scattered widely apart. It appears from a consideration of the present positions of the fragments that they were originally in the upper chambers of the palace, and have fallen on the destruction of the building. In some of the lower chambers they lay covering the whole floor, in other cases they lay in groups or patches on the pavement, and there are occasional clusters of fragments at various heights in the earth which covers the buildings. The other fragments are scattered singly through all the upper earth which covers the floors and walls of the palace. Different fragments of the same tablets and cylinders are found in separate chambers which have no immediate connection with each other, showing that the present distribution of the fragments has nothing to do with the original position of the tablets.

A consideration of the inscriptions shows that these tablets have been arranged according to their subjects in various positions in the libraries. Stories or subjects were commenced on tablets and continued on other tablets of the same size and form, in some cases the number of tablets in a series and on a single subject amounting to over one hundred.

Each subject or series of tablets had a title, the title being formed by the first phrase or part of phrase in the subject. Thus, the series of Astrological tablets, numbering over seventy tablets, bore the

title "When the gods Anu, Elu," this being the
commencement of the first tablet.   At the end of
every tablet in each series was written its number in
the work, thus: "the first tablet of When the gods
Anu, Elu," the second tablet of "When the gods
Anu, Elu," &c. &c.; and, further to preserve the
proper position of each tablet, every one except the
last in a series had at the end a catch phrase, consisting of the first line of the following tablet.   There
were beside, catalogues of these documents written
like them on clay tablets, and other small oval
tablets with titles upon them, apparently labels for
the various series of works.   All these arrangements
show the care taken with respect to literary matters.
There were regular libraries or chambers, probably
on the upper floors of the palaces, appointed for the
store of the tablets, and custodians or librarians to
take charge of them.   It is probable that all these
regulations were of great antiquity, and were copied
like the tablets from the Babylonians.

Judging from the fragments discovered, it appears.
probable that there were in the Royal Library at
Nineveh over 10,000 inscribed tablets, including
almost every subject in ancient literature.

In considering a subject like the present one it is
a point of the utmost importance to define as closely
as possible the date of our present copies of the
legends, and the most probable period at which the
original copies may have been inscribed.   By far the
greatest number of the tablets brought from Nineveh

belong to the age of Assurbanipal, who reigned over
Assyria B.C. 670, and every copy of the Genesis
legends yet found was inscribed during his reign.
The statements on the present tablets are conclusive
on this point, and have not been called in question,
but it is equally stated and acknowledged on all
hands that these tablets are not the originals, but are
only copies from earlier texts. It is unfortunate that
the date of the original copies is never preserved, and
thus a wide door is thrown open for difference of
opinion on this point. The Assyrians acknowledge
themselves that this literature was borrowed from
Babylonian sources, and of course it is to Babylonia
we have to look to ascertain the approximate dates
of the original documents. The difficulty here is
increased by the following considerations: it appears
that at an early period in Babylonian history a great
literary development took place, and numerous works
were produced which embodied the prevailing myths,
religion, and science of that day. Written many of
them in a noble style of poetry, and appealing to the
strongest feelings of the people on one side, or regis-
tering the highest efforts of their science on the
other, these texts became the standards for Babylonian literature, and later generations were content
to copy these writings instead of making new works
for themselves. Clay, the material on which they
were written, was everywhere abundant, copies were
multiplied, and by the veneration in which they
were held these texts fixed and stereotyped the style

of Babylonian literature, and the language in which they were written remained the classical style in the country down to the Persian conquest. Thus it happens that texts of Rim-agu, Sargon, and Hammurabi, who were one thousand years before Nebuchadnezzar and Nabonidus, show the same language as the texts of these later kings, there being no sensible difference in style to match the long interval between them.

There is, however, reason to believe that, although the language of devotion and literature remained fixed, the speech of the bulk of the people was gradually modified; and in the time of Assurbanipal, when, the Assyrians copied the Genesis legends, the common speech of the day was in very different style. The private letters and despatches of this age which have been discovered differ widely from the language of the contemporary public documents and religious writings, showing the change the language had undergone since the style of these was fixed. We have a slightly similar case in England, where the language of devotion and the style of the Bible differ in several respects from those of the English of to-day.

These considerations show the difficulty of fixing the age of a document from its style, and the difficulty is further increased by the uncertainty which hangs over all Babylonian chronology.

Chronology is always a thorny subject, and dry and unsatisfactory to most persons beside; some notice must, however, be taken of it here, in order to show the reasons for the dates and epochs fixed upon for the Genesis legends.

In this case the later chronology is not in question, and it is best to start with the generally received date of about B.C. 1300 for the conquest of Babylonia by Tugultininip, king of Assyria. Before this date we have a period of about 250 years, during which a foreign race ruled at Babylon. Berosus calls these foreigners Arabs, but nothing is known as to their original home or race. It is supposed that this race came into Babylonia, or obtained dominion there under a king named Hammurabi, whose date is thus fixed about B.C. 1550. Many scholars do not agree to this, and consider Hammurabi much more ancient; no one, however, fixes him later than the sixteenth century B.C., so that the date B.C. 1550 may be accepted as the most moderate one possible for the epoch of Hammurabi. The date of Hammurabi is of consequence in the question, because there is no evidence of these legends being written after his epoch.

This circumstance may be accounted for by the fact that during the period following the conquest of Hammurabi the government was in the hands of foreigners, and was much more centralized than it had been before, Babylon being, so far as we know, the sole capital, the great cities which had been centres of literature suffering a decline.

Before the time of Hammurabi, there ruled several

races of kings, of whom we possess numerous monuments. These monarchs principally reigned at the cities of Ur, Karrak, Larsa, and Akkad. Their inscriptions do not determine the length of their rule, but they probably covered the period from B.C. 2000 to 1550. The name of the monarch in whose time we have the first satisfactory evidence of contemporary monuments is read Urukh, and in the present state of our researches he may be fixed B.C. 2000. It must, however, be remarked that many scholars place him at a much earlier date. From the time of Urukh to that of Hammurabi the title of honour principally taken by the kings is " King of Sumir and Akkad," that is, King of Lower and Upper Babylonia. It appears probable that previous to the reign of Urukh the two divisions of Sumir and Akkad were separate monarchies; and it is therefore likely that any literature written before B.C. 2000 will show evidences of this division.

The rough outlines of Babylonian chronology at this period may be arranged as follows, always bearing in mind that the different dates are the lowest we can fairly assume, and that several of them may be much more ancient :—

Down to B.C. 2000 epoch of independent kingdoms in Babylonia; the principal centre of activity being Akkad, a region on the Euphrates, somewhere between latitudes 32° and 33°.

B.C. 2000. Era of Urukh, king of Ur, rise of Sumir, the southern part of the country, Ur the metropolis.

B.C. 1850. Era of Ismi-dagan, king of Karrak, Karrak the metropolis.

B.C. 1700. Rise of Larsa as metropolis.

B.C. 1600. Era of Sargon, king of Akkad; revival of the power of Akkad.

B.C. 1550. Era of Hammurabi, king of Babylon. Babylon the metropolis.

Although we cannot fix the dates of any monuments before the time of Urukh, B.C. 2000, it is quite certain that there were buildings and inscriptions before that date; and there are two literary works which I should judge to be certainly older than this epoch, namely, the great Chaldean work on Astrology, and a legend which, for want of a better title, I call the Exploits of Lubara.

The Chaldean work, containing the bulk of their astrology, appears to belong to the northern half of the country, that is to Akkad, and always speaks of Akkad as a separate state, and implies it to be the leading state. It mentions besides, the kingdoms of Subartu, Martu, or Syria, Gutim or Goim, and Elam, and some parts, perhaps of later date than the body of the work, give also the kingdoms of Kassi, Kissati, or the peoples, Nituk or Asmun, Sumir, Yamutbal, and Assan. In the body of the work there appear glosses, apparently later additions, mentioning kings of the period B.C. 2000 to 1850. I have not noticed any gloss containing a royal name later than the kings of Ur.

The work I have provisionally called " The Exploits of Lubara," and which also bears evidence of great antiquity, is a much shorter one, for while there are over seventy large tablets of the astrology, this, on the other hand, only contained five small tablets. This work notices a large number of peoples or states, the principal being the people of the coast, Subartu, Assyria, Elam, Kassi, Sutu, Goim, Lullubu, Akkad; the uniting of Sumir and Akkad, which was accomplished at least B.C. 2000, is not mentioned, but the notice of the Assyrians is rather an argument for a later date than I have chosen.

The Izdubar legends, containing the story of the Flood, and what I believe to be the history of Nimrod, were probably written in the south of the country, and at least as early as B.C. 2000. These legends were, however, traditions before they were committed to writing, and were common in some form to all the country. The story of the Creation and Fall belongs to the upper or Akkad division of the country, and may not have been committed to writing so early as the Izdubar legends; but even this is of great antiquity.

About the same time as the account of the Creation, a series of tablets on evil spirits, which contained a totally different tradition of the Creation, was probably written; and there is a third account from the City of Cutha, closely agreeing in some respects with the account handed down by Berosus, which I should provisionally place about the same date. It seems, from the indications in the inscriptions, that there happened in the interval B.C. 2000 to 1850 a general collecting and development of the various traditions of the Creation, Flood, Tower of Babel, and other similar legends.

A little later, about B.C. 1600, a new set of astrological tablets was written, together with a long work on terrestrial omens; these appear to belong to the kingdom and period of Sargon, king of Akkad.

Some at least, and probably most of the syllabaries, bilingual and explanatory tablets, grammars and vocabularies, belong to this period also; but a few are of later date.

In spite of the indications as to peculiarities of worship, names of states and capitals, historical allusions and other evidence, it may seem hazardous to many persons to fix the dates of original documents so high, when our only copies in many cases are Assyrian transcripts made in the reign of Assurbanipal, in the seventh century B.C.; but one or two considerations may show that this is a perfectly reasonable view, and no other likely period can be found for the original composition of the documents unless we ascend to a greater antiquity. In the first place, it must be noticed that the Assyrians themselves state that the documents were copied from ancient Babylonian copies, and in some cases state that the old copies were partly illegible even in their day. Again, in one case there is actual proof of the antiquity of a text, an Assyrian copy of part of which is published in "Cuneiform Inscriptions," vol. ii. plate 54, Nos.

3 & 4. In a collection of tablets discovered by Mr. Loftus at Senkereh, belonging, according to the kings mentioned in it, to about B.C. 1600, is part of an ancient Babylonian copy of this very text, the Babylonian copy being about one thousand years older than the Assyrian one.

It is, however, probable that most of the legends treated of in the present volume had existed as traditions in the country long before they were committed to writing, and some of these traditions, as embodied in the various works, exhibit great difference in ·details, showing that they had passed through many changes.

Taking the period of literary development in Babylonia as extending from B.C. 2000 to 1550, we may say, it roughly synchronizes with the period from Abraham to Moses, according to the ordinary chronology of our Bibles, and during this period it appears that traditions of the creation of the universe, and human history down to the time of Nimrod, existed parallel to, and in some points identical with, those given in the Book of Genesis.

Many of the documents embodying these traditions have been discovered in sadly mutilated condition, but there can be no doubt that future explorations will reveal more perfect copies, and numerous companion and explanatory texts, which will one day clear up the difficulties which now meet us at every step of their consideration.

So far as known contemporary inscriptions are

concerned, we cannot consider our present researches
and discoveries as anything like sufficient to give a
fair view of the literature of Assyria and Babylonia,
and, however numerous and important are the Genesis
legends, they form but a small portion of the whole
literature of the country.

It is generally considered that the earliest inscriptions of any importance which we now possess belong
to the time of Urukh, king of Ur, whose age may be
placed with great probability about two thousand
years before the Christian era.

The principal inscriptions of this period consist of
texts on bricks and on signet cylinders, and some of
the latter may be of much greater antiquity.   Passing
down to the period of the kingdoms of Karrak, Larsa,
and Akkad, we find a great accession of literary
material, almost every class of writing being represented by contemporary specimens.   It is certain
that even then the inscribed clay tablets were not
isolated, but already they were arranged in collections or libraries, and these collections were placed at
some of the principal cities.   From Senkerch and its
neighbourhood have come our earliest specimens of
these literary tablets, the following being some of the
contents of this earliest known library :—

1. Mythological tablets, including lists of the gods,
and their manifestations and titles.

2. Grammatical works, lists of words, and explanations.

3. Mathematical works, calculations, tables, cube
and square root, measures.

4. Astronomy, astrology, and omens.

5. Legends and short historical inscriptions.

6. Historical cylinders, one of Kudur-mabuk, B.C. 1600 (the earliest known cylinder), being in the British Museum.

7. Geographical tablets, and lists of towns and countries.

8. Laws and law cases, sale and barter, wills and loans.

Such are the inscriptions from the libraries of the early inhabitants of Babylonia, and beside these there are numérous texts, only known to us through later copies, but which certainly had their origin as early as this period.

Passing down from this period, for some centuries we find only detached inscriptions, accompanied by evidence of the gradual shifting both of the political power and literary activity from Babylonia to Assyria.

In Assyria the first centre of Literature and seat of a library was the city of Assur (Kileh Shergat), and the earliest known tablets date about B.C. 1500.

Beyond the scanty records of some of the monarchs nothing of value remains of this library for several centuries, and the Assyrian literary works are only known from later copies.

A revival of the Assyrian empire began under Assur-nazir-pal, king of Assyria, who ascended the throne B.C. 885. He rebuilt the city of Calah (Nimroud), and this city became the seat of an Assyrian library. Tablets were procured from Babylonia by

Shalmaneser, son of Assur-nazir-pal, B.C. 860, during
the reign of Nabu-bal-idina, king of Babylon, and these
were copied by the Assyrian scribes, and placed in
the royal library. Vul-nirari, grandson of Shalmaneser, B.C. 812, added to the Calah library, and had
tablets written at Nineveh. Assurnirari, B.C. 755,
continued the literary work, some mythological
tablets being dated in his reign.

Tiglath Pileser, B.C. 745, enlarged the library, and
placed in it various copies of historical inscriptions.
It was, however, reserved for Sargon, who founded
the last Assyrian dynasty, B.C. 722, to make the
Assyrian royal library worthy of the empire. Early
in his reign he appointed Nabu-suqub-gina principal
librarian, and this officer set to work making new
copies of all the standard works of the day. During
the whole of his term of office copies of the great
literary works were produced, the majority of the
texts preserved belonging to the early period previous
to B.C. 1600.

In the period which followed there was a general
revival of all the ancient works which had escaped
destruction, and the study of this early literature
became a marked feature of the time.

Sennacherib, son of Sargon, B.C. 705, continued to
add to his father's library at Calah, but late in his
reign he removed the collection from that city to
Nineveh, where from this time the national library
remained until the fall of the empire.

Esarhaddon, son of Sennacherib, B.C. 681, further

increased the national collection, most of his works being of a religious character.

Assurbanipal, son of Esarhaddon, the Sardanapalus of the Greeks, B.C. 673, was the greatest of the Assyrian sovereigns, and he is far more memorable on account of his magnificent patronage of learning than on account of the greatness of his empire or the extent of his wars.

Assurbanipal added more to the Assyrian royal library than all the kings who had gone before him, and it is to tablets written in his reign that we owe almost all our knowledge of the Babylonian myths and early history, beside many other important matters.

The agents of Assurbanipal sought everywhere for inscribed tablets, brought them to Nineveh, and copied them there; thus the literary treasures of Babylon, Borsippa, Cutha, Akkad, Ur, Erech, Larsa, Nipur and various other cities were transferred to the Assyrian capital to enrich the great collection there.

The fragments brought over to Europe give us a good idea of this library and show the range of the subjects embraced by this collection of inscriptions. Among the different classes of texts, the Genesis stories and similar legends occupied a prominent place; these, as they will be further described in the present volume, need only be mentioned here. Accompanying them we have a series of mythological tablets of various sorts, varying from legends of the

D

gods, psalms, songs, prayers, and hymns, down to
mere allusions and lists of names. Many of these
texts take the form of charms to be used in sickness
and for the expulsion of evil spirits; some of them
are of great antiquity, being at least as old as the
creation and Izdubar legends. One fine series con-
cerns the cure of witchcraft, a superstition fully
believed in in those days. Izdubar is mentioned in
one of these tablets as lord of the oaths or pledges
of the world.

Some of the prayers were for use on special occa-
sions, such as on starting on a campaign, on the
occurrence of an eclipse, &c. Astronomy and
Astrology were represented by various detached
inscriptions and reports, but principally by the great
work on these subjects covering over seventy tablets
which was borrowed from the early Chaldeans, and
many copies of which were in the Library of Assurbanipal. This work on Astrology and Astronomy
was, as I have already stated, one of the most ancient
texts in the Euphrates valley.

There were also numerous copies of a long work
on Terrestrial omens, which appears to date from
the time of Sargon, king of Akkad, about B.C. 1600.
In this work everything in nature is supposed to
portend some coming event.

There is a fragment of one Astrological tablet
which professes to be copied from an original of the
time of Izdubar.

Historical texts formed another section of the

library, and these included numerous copies of inscriptions of early Babylonian kings; there were beside, chronological tablets with lists of kings and annual officers, inscriptions of various Assyrian monarchs, histories of the relations between Assyria and Babylonia, Elam, and Arabia, treaties, despatches, proclamations, and reports on the state of the empire and military affairs.

Natural history was represented by tables of animals; mammals, birds, reptiles, fishes, insects, and plants, trees, grasses, reeds, and grains, earths, stones, &c. These lists are classified according to the supposed nature and affinities of the various species, and show considerable advance in the sciences. Mathematics had a place in the library, there being problems, figures, and calculations; but this branch of learning was not studied so fully as in Babylonia.

Grammar and Lexicography were better represented, there being many works on these subjects, including lists of the signs and explanations, declension of nouns, conjugation of verbs, examples of syntax, bilingual tables, explanatory lists, &c. All these tablets were copied from the Babylonians. In law and civil matters the library was also rich, and the tablets serve to show that the same laws and customs prevailed in Assyria as in Babylonia. There are codes of laws, law cases, sale, barter, loans, lists of property, lists of titles and trades, tribute, and taxes, &c.

In Geography the Assyrians were not very forward;

but there are lists of countries and their productions, of cities, rivers, mountains, and peoples.

Such are some of the principal contents of the great library from which we have obtained our copies of the Creation and Flood legends, most of the tablets were copied from early Babylonian inscriptions, the original copies of the works have in most cases disappeared; but these remarkable inscriptions have preserved to us texts which show the wonderful advance made by the people of Chaldea before the time of Moses. Babylonian literature, which had been the parent of Assyrian writing, revived after the fall of Nineveh, and Nebuchadnezzar and his successors made Babylon the seat of a library rivalling that of Assurbanipal at Nineveh. Of this later development of Babylonian literature we know very little, explorations being still required to bring to light the texts of this epoch. Few fragments only, discovered by wandering Arabs or recovered by chance travellers, have yet turned up, but there is in them evidence enough to promise a rich reward to future excavators.

Chapter III.

CHALDEAN LEGENDS TRANSMITTED THROUGH BEROSUS AND OTHER ANCIENT AUTHORS.

Berosus and his copyists.—Cory's translation.—Alexander Polyhistor.—Babylonia.—Oannes, his teaching.—Creation.—Belus.—Chaldean kings.—Xisuthrus.—Deluge.—The Ark.—Return to Babylon.—Apollodorus.—Pantibiblon.—Larancha.—Abydenus.—Alorus, first king.—Ten kings.—Sisithrus.—Deluge.—Armenia.—Tower of Babel.—Cronos and Titan.—Nicolaus Damascenus.—Dispersion from Hestiæus.—Babylonian colonies.—Tower of Babel.—The Sibyl.—Titan and Prometheus.—Damascius.—Tauthe.—Moymis.—Kissare and Assorus.—Triad.—Bel.

 HAVE included in this chapter the principal extracts from ancient authors respecting the Babylonian accounts of Genesis. Many others are known, but are of doubtful origin, and of less immediate interest to my subject.

Berosus, from whom the principal extracts are copied, lived, as I have mentioned in Chapter I., about B.C. 330 to 260, and, from his position as a

Babylonian priest, had the best means of knowing the Babylonian traditions.

The others are later writers, who copied in the main from Berosus, and whose notices may be taken as giving abridgments of his statements.

I have preferred as usual, the translations of Cory as being standard ones, and made without prejudice from recent discoveries.

EXTRACT I. FROM ALEXANDER POLYHISTOR
(CORY, p. 21).

Berosus, in the first book of his history of Babylonia, informs us that he lived in the age of Alexander, the son of Philip. And he mentions that there were written accounts, preserved at Babylon with the greatest care, comprehending a period of above fifteen myriads of years; and that these writings contained histories of the heaven and of the sea; of the birth of mankind; and of the kings, and of the memorable actions which they had achieved.

And in the first place he describes Babylonia as a country situated between the Tigris and the Euphrates; that it abounded with wheat, and barley, and ocrus, and sesame; and that in the lakes were produced the roots called gongæ, which are fit for food, and in respect to nutriment similar to barley. That there were also palm-trees and apples, and a variety of fruits; fish also and birds, both those which are merely of flight, and those which frequent the lakes. He adds that those parts of the country which bordered upon Arabia were without water, and barren; but that the parts which lay on the other side were both hilly and fertile.

At Babylon there was (in these times) a great resort of people of various nations, who inhabited Chaldea, and lived in a lawless manner like the beasts of the field.

In the first year there appeared, from that part of the Erythræan sea which borders upon Babylonia, an animal endowed with reason, by name Oannes,

OANNES AND OTHER BABYLONIAN MYTHOLOGICAL FIGURES
FROM CYLINDER.

whose whole body (according to the account of Apollodorus) was that of a fish; that under the fish's head he had another head, with feet also below similar to those of a man, subjoined to the fish's tail. His voice, too, and language were articulate and human; and a representation of him is preserved even to this day.

This being was accustomed to pass the day among men, but took no food at that season; and he gave them an insight into letters and sciences, and arts of every kind. He taught them to construct cities, to found temples, to compile laws, and explained to them the principles of geometrical knowledge. He made them distinguish the seeds of the earth, and showed them how to collect the fruits; in short, he instructed them in every thing which could tend to soften manners and humanize their lives. From that time, nothing material has been added by way of improvement to his instructions. And when the sun had set this being Oannes retired again into the sea, and passed the night in the deep, for he was amphibious. After this there appeared other animals like Oannes, of which Berosus proposes to give an account when he comes to the history of the kings. Moreover, Oannes wrote concerning the generation of mankind, and of their civil polity; and the following is the purport of what he said :—

" There was a time in which there existed nothing but darkness and an abyss of waters, wherein resided most hideous beings, which were produced of a two-fold principle. There appeared men, some of whom were furnished with two wings, others with four, and with two faces. They had one body, but two heads; the one that of a man, the other of a woman; and likewise in their several organs both male and female. Other human figures were to be seen with the legs and horns of a goat; some had horses' feet, while others united the hind quarters of a horse with the body of a man, resembling in shape the hippocentaurs. Bulls likewise were bred there with the heads of men; and dogs with fourfold bodies, terminated in their extremities with the tails of fishes; horses also with the heads of dogs; men, too, and other animals, with the heads and bodies of horses, and the tails of fishes. In short, there were creatures in which were combined the limbs of every species of animals. In addition to these, fishes, reptiles, serpents, with other monstrous animals, which assumed each other's shape and countenance.

COMPOSITE ANIMALS FROM CYLINDER.

Of all which were preserved delineations in the temple of Belus at Babylon.

"The person who presided over them was a woman named Omoroca, which in the Chaldean language is Thalatth, in Greek Thalassa, the sea; but which might equally be interpreted the moon. All things being in this situation, Belus came, and cut the woman asunder, and of one half of her he formed the earth, and of the other half the heavens, and at the same time destroyed the animals within her (or in the abyss).

"All this" (he says) "was an allegorical description of nature. For, the whole universe consisting of moisture, and animals being continually generated therein, the deity above-mentioned took off his own head; upon which the other gods mixed the blood, as it gushed out, and from thence formed men. On this account it is that they are rational, and partake of divine knowledge. This Belus, by whom they signify Jupiter, divided the darkness, and separated the heavens from the earth, and reduced the universe to order. But the animals, not being able to bear the prevalence of light, died. Belus upon this, seeing a vast space unoccupied, though by nature fruitful, commanded one of the gods to take off his head, and to mix the blood with the earth, and from thence to form other men and animals, which should be capable of bearing the air. Belus formed also the stars, and the sun, and the moon, and the five planets." (Such, according to Polyhistor Alexander, is the account which Berosus gives in his first book.)

(In the second book was contained the history of the ten kings of the Chaldeans, and the periods of the continuance of each reign, which consisted collectively of an hundred and twenty sari, or four hundred and thirty-two thousand years; reaching to the time of the Deluge. For Alexander, enumerating the kings from the writings of the Chaldeans, after the ninth Ardates, proceeds to the tenth, who is called by them Xisuthrus, in this manner) :—

"After the death of Ardates, his son Xisuthrus reigned eighteen sari. In his time happened a great deluge; the history of which is thus described. The deity Cronos appeared to him in a vision, and warned him that upon the fifteenth day of the month Dæsius there would be a flood, by which mankind would be destroyed. He therefore enjoined him to write a history of the beginning, procedure, and conclusion of all things, and to bury it in the city of the Sun at Sippara; and to build a vessel, and take with him into it his friends and relations; and to convey on board every thing necessary to sustain life, together with all the different animals, both birds and quadrupeds, and trust himself fearlessly to the deep. Having asked the Deity whither he was to sail, he was answered, ' To the Gods;' upon which he offered up a prayer for the good of mankind. He then obeyed the divine admonition, and built a vessel five stadia in length, and two in breadth. Into this he put everything which he had prepared, and last of all conveyed into it his wife, his children, and his friends.

After the flood had been upon the earth, and was in time abated, Xisuthrus sent out birds from the vessel; which not finding any food, nor any place whereupon they might rest their feet, returned to him again. After an interval of some days, he sent them forth a second time; and they now returned with their feet tinged with mud. He made a trial a third time with these birds; but they returned to him no more: from whence he judged that the surface of the earth had appeared above the waters.

He therefore made an opening in the vessel, and upon looking out found that it was stranded upon the side of some mountain; upon which he immediately quitted it with his wife, his daughter, and the pilot. Xisuthrus then paid his adoration to the earth : and, having constructed an altar, offered sacrifices to the gods, and, with those who had come out of the vessel with him, disappeared.

They, who remained within, finding that their companions did not return, quitted the vessel with many lamentations, and called continually on the name of Xisuthrus. Him they saw no more ; but they could distinguish his voice in the air, and could hear him admonish them to pay due regard to religion; and likewise informed them that it was upon account of his piety that he was translated to live with the gods, that his wife and daughter and the pilot had obtained the same honour. To this he added that they should return to Babylonia, and, as it was ordained, search for the writings at Sippara, which they were to make known to all mankind; moreover, that the place wherein they then were was the land of Armenia. The rest having heard these words offered sacrifices to the gods, and, taking a circuit, journeyed towards Babylonia.

The vessel being thus stranded in Armenia, some part of it yet remains in the Corcyræan mountains of Armenia, and the people scrape off the bitumen with which it had been outwardly coated, and make use of it by way of an alexipharmic and amulet.

And when they returned to Babylon and had found the writings at Sippara they built cities and erected temples, and Babylon was thus inhabited again.— *Syncel. Chron.* xxviii.; *Euseb. Chron.* v. 8.

BEROSUS, FROM APOLLODORUS (CORY, p. 30).

This is the history which Berosus has transmitted to us. He tells us that the first king was Alorus of Babylon, a Chaldean, he reigned ten sari; and afterwards Alaparus and Amelon, who came from Pantebiblon; then Ammenon the Chaldean, in whose time appeared the Musarus Oannes, the Annedotus from the Erythræan sea. (But Alexander Polyhistor, anticipating the event, has said that he appeared in the first year, but Apollodorus says that it was after forty sari; Abydenus, however, makes the second Annedotus appear after twenty-six sari.) Then succeeded Megalarus from the city of Pantibiblon, and he reigned eighteen sari; and after him Daonus, the shepherd from Pantibiblon, reigned ten sari; in his time (he says) appeared again from the Erythræan sea a fourth Annedotus, having the same form with those above, the shape of a fish blended with that of a man. Then reigned Euedorachus from Pantibiblon for the term of eighteen sari; in his days there appeared another personage from the Erythræan sea like the former, having the same complicated form between a fish and a man, whose name was Odacon. (All these, says Apollodorus, related particularly and circumstantially whatever Oannes had informed them of; concerning these Abydenus has made no mention.) Then reigned Amempsinus, a Chaldean from Larancha; and he being the eighth in order reigned ten sari. Then reigned Otiartes, a Chaldean, from Larancha; and he reigned eight sari. And, upon the death of Otiartes, his son Xisuthrus reigned eighteen sari; in his time happened the great Deluge. So that the sum of all the kings is ten; and the term which they collectively reigned an hundred and twenty sari.—*Syncel. Chron.* xxxix.; *Euseb. Chron.* v.

BEROSUS, FROM ABYDENUS (CORY, p. 32).

So much concerning the wisdom of the Chaldeans.

It is said that the first king of the country was Alorus, and that he gave out a report that God had appointed him to be the shepherd of the people, he reigned ten sari; now a sarus is esteemed to be three thousand six hundred years, a neros six hundred, and a sossus sixty.

After him Alaparus reigned three sari; to him succeeded Amillarus from the city of Pantibiblon, who reigned thirteen sari; in his time came up from the sea a second Annedotus, a semi-demon very similar in his form to Oannes; after Amillarus reigned Ammenon twelve sari, who was of the city of Pantibiblon; then Megalarus of the same place reigned eighteen sari; then Daos the shepherd governed for the space of ten sari, he was of Pantibiblon; in his time four double-shaped personages came up out of the sea to land, whose names were Euedocus, Eneugamus, Eneuboulus, and Anementus; afterwards in the time of Euedoreschus appeared another, Anodaphus. After these reigned other kings, and last of all Sisithrus, so that in the whole the number amounted to ten kings, and the term of their reigns to an hundred and twenty sari. (And among other things not irrelative to the subject he continues thus concerning the Deluge): After Euedoreschus some others reigned, and then Sisithrus. To him the deity Cronos foretold that on the fifteenth day of the month Dæsius there would be a deluge of rain: and he commanded him to deposit all the writings whatever which were in his possession in the city of the sun in Sippara. Sisithrus, when he had complied with these commands, sailed immediately to Armenia, and was presently inspired by God. Upon the third day after the cessation of the rain Sisithrus sent out birds by way of experiment, that he might judge whether the flood had subsided. But the birds, passing over an unbounded sea without finding any place of rest, returned again to Sisithrus. This he repeated with other birds. And when upon the third trial he succeeded, for the birds then returned with their feet stained with mud, the gods translated him from among men. With respect to the vessel, which yet remains in Armenia, it is a custom of the inhabitants to form bracelets and amulets of its wood.— *Syncel. Chron.* xxxviii.; *Euseb. Præp. Evan.* lib. ix.; *Euseb. Chron.* v. 8.

Of the Tower of Babel (Cory, p. 34).

They say that the first inhabitants of the earth, glorying in their own strength and size and despising the gods, undertook to raise a tower whose top should reach the sky, in the place in which Babylon now stands; but when it approached the heaven the winds assisted the gods, and overthrew the work upon its contrivers, and its ruins are said to be still at Babylon; and the gods introduced a diversity of tongues among men, who till that time had all spoken the same language; and a war arose between Cronos and Titan. The place in which they built the tower is now called Babylon on account of the confusion of tongues, for confusion is by the Hebrews called Babel.—*Euseb. Præp. Evan.* lib. ix.; *Syncel. Chron.* xliv.; *Euseb. Chron.* xiii.

Of the Ark, from Nicolaus Damascenus (Cory, p. 49).

There is above Minyas in the land of Armenia a very great mountain which is called Baris, to which it is said that many persons retreated at the time of the Deluge and were saved, and that one in particular was carried thither in an ark and was landed on its summit, and that the remains of the vessel were long preserved upon the mountain. Perhaps this was the same individual of whom Moses, the legislator of the Jews, has made mention.—*Jos. Ant. Jud.* i. 3; *Euseb. Præp. Evan.* ix.

OF THE DISPERSION, FROM HESTLÆUS (CORY, p. 50).

The priests who escaped took with them the imple-ments of the worship of the Enyalian Jove, and came to Senaar in Babylonia. But they were again driven from thence by the introduction of a diversity of tongues; upon which they founded colonies in various parts, each settling in such situations as chance or the direction of God led them to occupy.—*Jos. Ant. Jud.* i. c. 4; *Euseb. Præp. Evan.* ix.

OF THE TOWER OF BABEL, FROM ALEXANDER POLY-HISTOR (CORY, p. 50).

The Sibyl says: That when all men formerly spoke the same language some among them undertook to erect a large and lofty tower, that they might climb up into heaven. But God sending forth a whirlwind confounded their design, and gave to each tribe a particular language of its own, which is the reason that the name of that city is Babylon. After the deluge lived Titan and Prometheus, when Titan undertook a war against Cronus.—*Sync.* xliv.; *Jos. Ant. Jud.* i. c. 4; *Euseb. Præp. Evan.* ix.

THE THEOGONIES, FROM DAMASCIUS (CORY, p. 318).

But the Babyolnians, like the rest of the barba-rians, pass over in silence the One principle of the universe, and they constitute two, Tauthe and Apa-son, making Apason the husband of Tauthe, and

E

denominating her the mother of the gods. And from these proceeds an only-begotten son, Moymis, which I conceive is no other than the intelligible world proceeding from the two principles. From them also another progeny is derived, Dache and Dachus; and again a third, Kissare and Assorus, from which last three others proceed, Anus, and Illinus, and Aus. And of Aus and Davce is born a son called Belus, who, they say, is the fabricator of the world, the Demiurgus.

CHAPTER IV.

BABYLONIAN MYTHOLOGY.

Greek accounts.—Mythology local in origin.—Antiquity.—
Conquests.—Colonies.—Three great gods.—Twelve great gods.
—Angels.—Spirits.—Anu.—Anatu.—Vul.—Ishtar.—Equiva-
lent to Venus.—Hea.—Oannes.—Merodach.—Bel or Jupiter.—
Zirat-banit, Succoth Benoth.—Elu.—Sin the moon god.—Ninip.
—Shamas.—Nergal.—Anunit.—Table of gods.

IN their accounts of the Creation and of
the early history of the human race the
Babylonian divinities figure very prominently, but it is difficult in many cases
to identify the deities mentioned by the Greek
authors, because the phonetic reading of the names
of the Babylonian gods is very obscure, and the
classical writers often mention these divinities by the
terms in their own mythology, which appeared to
them to correspond with the Babylonian names.

In this chapter it is only proposed to give a
general account of some parts of the Babylonian
mythology, to show the relationship between the
deities and their titles and work.

Babylonian mythology was local in origin; each of the gods had a particular city which was the seat of his worship, and it is probable that the idea of weaving the gods into a system, in which each should have his part to play, only had its origin at a later time. The antiquity of this mythology may be seen by the fact, that two thousand years before the Christian era it was already completed, and its deities definitely connected into a system which remained with little change down to the close of the kingdom.

It is probable that the gods were in early times only worshipped at their original cities or seats, the various cities or settlements being independent of each other; but it was natural as wars arose, and some cities gained conquests over others, and kings gradually united the country into monarchies, that the people of conquering cities should claim that their gods were superior to those of the cities they conquered, and thus came the system of different ranks or grades among the gods. Again, colonies were sent out of some cities, and the colonies, as they considered themselves sons of the cities they started from, also considered their gods to be sons of the gods of the mother cities. Political changes in early times led to the rise and fall of various cities and consequently of their deities, and gave rise to numerous myths relating to the different personages in the mythology. In some remote age there appear to have been three great cities in the country, Erech, Eridu, and Nipur, and their divinities Anu, Hea, and Bel were considered

the "great gods" of the country. Subsequent
changes led to the decline of these cities, but their
deities still retained their position at the head of the
Babylonian system.

These three leading deities formed members of a
circle of twelve gods, also called great. These gods
and their titles are given as:

1. Anu, king of angels and spirits, lord of the
city of Erech.

2. Bel, lord of the world, father of the gods,
creator, lord of the city of Nipur.

3. Hea, maker of fate, lord of the deep, god of
wisdom and knowledge, lord of the city of
Eridu.

4. Sin, lord of crowns, maker of brightness, lord
of the city of Ur.

5. Merodach, just prince of the gods, lord of
birth, lord of the city of Babylon.

6. Vul, the strong god, lord of canals and atmosphere, lord of the city of Muru.

7. Shamas, judge of heaven and earth, director
of all, lord of the cities of Larsa and Sippara.

8. Ninip, warrior of the warriors of the gods,
destroyer of wicked, lord of the city of Nipur.

9. Nergal, giant king of war, lord of the city of
Cutha.

10. Nusku, holder of the golden sceptre, the lofty
god.

11. Belat, wife of Bel, mother of the great gods,
lady of the city of Nipur.

12. Ishtar, eldest of heaven and earth, raising the face of warriors.

Below these deities there was a large body of gods forming the bulk of the pantheon, and below these were arranged the Igege, or angels of heaven, and the Anunnaki, or angels of earth. Below these again came various classes of spirits or genii called Sedu, Vadukku, Ekimu, Gallu, and others; some of these were evil, some good.

The relationship of the various principal gods and their names, titles, and offices will be seen by the following remarks.

At the head of the Babylonian mythology stands a deity who was sometimes identified with the heavens, sometimes considered as the ruler and god of heaven. This deity is named Anu, his sign is the simple star, the symbol of divinity, and at other times the Maltese cross. Anu represents abstract divinity, and he appears as an original principle, perhaps as the original principle of nature. He represents the universe as the upper and lower regions, and when these were divided the upper region or heaven was called Anu, while the lower region or earth was called Anatu; Anatu being the female principle or wife of Anu. Anu is termed the old god, and the god of the whole of heaven and earth; one of the manifestations of Anu was as the two forms Lahma and Lahama, which probably correspond to the Greek forms Dache and Dachus, see p. 50. These forms are said to have sprung out of the original chaos, and they are followed by the two forms sar and kisar (the Kissare and Assorus of the Greeks), sar means the upper hosts or expanse, kisar the lower hosts or expanse; these are also forms of manifestations of Anu and his wife. Anu is also lord of the old city, and he bears the names Alalu and Papsukul. His titles generally indicate height, antiquity, purity, divinity, and he may be taken as the general type of divinity. Anu was originally worshipped at the city of Erech, which was called the city of Anu and Anatu, and the great temple there was called the "house of Anu," or the "house of heaven."

Anatu, the wife or consort of Anu, is generally only a female form of Anu, but is sometimes contrasted with him; thus, when Anu represents height and heaven, Anatu represents depth and earth; she is also lady of darkness, the mother of the god Hea, the mother producing heaven and earth, the female fish-god, and she is one of the many goddesses called Istar or Venus.

Anu and Anatu have a numerous family; among their sons are numbered Sar-ziri, the king of the desert, Latarak, Abgula, Kusu, and the air-god, whose name is uncertain. The air-god is usually called Vul, he has also the name Pur, and the epithets Ramman or Rimmon, the self-existent, and Uban or Ben. Vul is god of the region of the atmosphere, or space between the heaven and earth, he is the god of rain, of storms and whirlwind, of thunder and lightning, of floods and watercourses. Vul was in high esteem in Syria and Arabia, where he bore the name of Daddi; in Armenia he was called Teiseba. Vul is always considered an active deity, and was extensively worshipped.

Another important god, a son of Anu, was the god of fire; his name may be read Bil-kan, with the possibility of some connection with the Biblical Tubal Cain and the classical Vulcan. The fire-god takes an active part in the numerous mythological tablets and legends, and he is considered to be the most potent deity in relation to witchcraft and spells generally.

The most important of the daughters of Anu was named Istar; she was in some respects the equivalent of the classical Venus. Her worship was at first subordinate to that of Anu, and as she was goddess of love, while Anu was god of heaven, it is probable that the first intention in the mythology was only to represent love as heaven-born; but in time a more sensual view prevailed, and the worship of Istar became one of the darkest features in Babylonian mythology. As the worship of this goddess increased in favour, it gradually superseded that of Anu, until in time his temple, the house of heaven, came to be regarded as the temple of Venus.

The planet Venus, as the evening star, was identified with the Ishtar of Erech, while the morning star was Anunit, goddess of Akkad.

There were various other goddesses called Istar, among which may be noticed Istar, daughter of Sin the moon-god, who is sometimes confounded with the daughter of Anu.

A companion deity with Anu is Hea, who is god of the sea and of Hades, in fact of all the lower regions. He has two features, and corresponds in some respects to the Saturn or Cronos of the ancients, in others to their Poseidon or Neptune. Hea is called god of the lower region, he is lord of the sea or abyss; he is lord of generation and of all human beings, he bears the titles lord of wisdom, of mines and treasures; he is lord of gifts, of music, of fishermen and sailors, and of Hades or hell. It has been supposed that the serpent was one of his emblems, and that he was the Oannes of Berosus; these things do not, however, appear in the inscriptions. The wife of Hea was Dav-kina, the Davke of Damascius, who is the goddess of the lower regions, the consort of the deep; and their principal son was Maruduk or Merodach, the Bel of later times.

Merodach, god of Babylon, appears in all the earlier inscriptions as the agent of his father Hea; he goes about in the world collecting information, and receives commissions from his father to set right all that appears wrong. Merodach is an active agent in creation, but is always subordinate to his father Hea. In later times, after Babylon had been made the capital, Merodach, who was god of that city, was raised to the head of the Pantheon. Merodach or Bel was identified with the classical Jupiter, but the name Bel, " the lord," was only given to him in times sub-

sequent to the rise of Babylon. The wife of Merodach was Zirat-banit, the Succoth Benoth of the
Bible.

Nebo, the god of knowledge and literature, who
was worshipped at the neighbouring city of Borsippa,
was a favourite deity in later times, as was also his
consort Tasmit. Beside Merodach Hea had a numerous progeny, his sons being principally river gods.

A third great god was united with Anu and Hea,
his names were Enu, Elu, Kaptu, and Bel; he was the
original Bel of the Babylonian mythology, and was
lord of the surface of the earth and the affairs of men.
Elu was lord of the city of Nipur, and had a consort
named Belat or Beltis. Elu, or Bel, is the most
active of the gods in the general affairs of mankind,
and was so generally worshipped in early times that
he came to be regarded as the national divinity, and
his temple at the city of Nipur was regarded as the
type of all temples. The extensive worship of Bel,
and the high honour in which he was held, seem to
point to a time when his city, Nipur, was the metropolis of the country.

Belat, or Beltis, the wife of Bel, is a famous deity
celebrated in all ages, but as the title Belat was
only "lady," or "goddess," it was a common one
for many goddesses, and the notices of Beltis probably refer to several different personages. The
same remark may be applied to the name Istar, or
Ishtar, meaning "goddess," which is applied to any
female divinity.

Elu had, like the other gods, a numerous family; his eldest son was the moon-god called Ur, Agu or Aku, Sin and Itu, in later times generally termed Sin. Sin was presiding deity of the city of Ur, and early assumed an important place in the mythology. The moon-god figures prominently in some early legends, and during the time the city of Ur was capital of the country his worship became very extensive and popular in the whole of the country.

Ninip, god of hunting and war, was another celebrated son of Elu; he was worshipped with his father at Nipur. Ninip was also much worshipped in Assyria as well as Babylonia, his character as presiding genius of war and the chase making him a favourite deity with the warlike kings of Assur.

Sin the moon-god had a son Shamas, or Samas, the sun-god, and a daughter, Istar or Venus. Shamas is an active deity in some of the Izdubar legends and fables, but he is generally subordinate to Sin. In the Babylonian system the moon takes precedence of the sun, and the Shamas of Larsa was probably considered a different deity to Shamas of Sippara.

Among the other deities of the Babylonians may be counted Nergal, god of Cutha, who, like Ninip, presided over hunting and war, and Anunit, the deity of one city of Sippara, and of the city of Akkad.

The following table will exhibit the relationship of the principal deities; but it must be noted that the

Assyrian inscriptions are not always consistent, either as to the sex or paternity of the gods :—

Tavtu   Absu (Apason ?)
(the sea).   (the deep).

Mummu
(chaos ?)

Lahma   Lahama
(force or growth).

Kisar (Kisare)   Sar (Assare)
(lower expanse).   (upper expanse).

Anu (Ouranus)   Anatu   Elu, or Bel.   Beltis.
(heaven).   (earth).

Vul   Bil-kan (Vulcan)   Hea (Saturn).   Istar (Venus).
(atmosphere).   (fire-god).

Hea (Saturn).   Davkina (Davke).   Elu.   Beltis.

Merodach.   Zirat-banit.   Sin.   Ningal.   Ninip.

Nebo.   Tasmit.   Samas.   Istar.

CHAPTER V.

BABYLONIAN LEGEND OF THE CREATION.

Mutilated condition of tablets.—List of subjects.—Description of chaos.—Tiamat.—Generation of gods.—Damascius.—Comparison with Genesis.—Three great gods.—Doubtful fragments.—Fifth tablet.—Stars.—Planets.—Moon.—Sun.—Abyss or chaos.—Creation of moon.—Creation of animals.—Man.—His duties.—Dragon of sea.—Fall.—Curse for disobedience.—Discussion.—Sacred tree.—Dragon or serpent.—War with Tiamat.—Weapons.—Merodach.—Destruction of Tiamat.—Mutilation of documents.—Parallel Biblical account.—Age of story.

I HAVE related in the first chapter the history of the discovery of this legend; the tablets composing it are in mutilated condition, and too fragmentary to enable a single tablet to be completed, or to give more than a general view of the whole subject. The story, so far as I can judge from the fragment, agrees generally with the account of the Creation in the Book of Genesis, but shows traces of having originally included very much more matter. The fragments of the story which I have arranged are as follows:—

1. Part of the first tablet, giving an account of the Chaos and the generation of the gods.

2: Fragment of subsequent tablet, perhaps the second on the foundation of the deep.

3. Fragment of tablet placed here with great doubt, probably referring to the creation of land.

4. Part of the fifth tablet, giving the creation of the heavenly bodies.

5. Fragment of seventh? tablet, giving the creation of land animals.

6. Fragments of three tablets on the creation and fall of man.

7. Fragments of tablets relating to the war between the gods and evil spirits.

These fragments indicate that the series included at least twelve tablets, the writing on each tablet being in one column on the front and back, and probably including over one hundred lines of text.

The first fragment in the story is the upper part of the first tablet, giving the description of the void or chaos, and part of the generation of the gods. The translation is:

1. When above, were not raised the heavens:

2. and below on the earth a plant had not grown up;

3. the abyss also had not broken open their boundaries:

4. The chaos (or water) Tiamat (the sea) was the producing-mother of the whole of them.

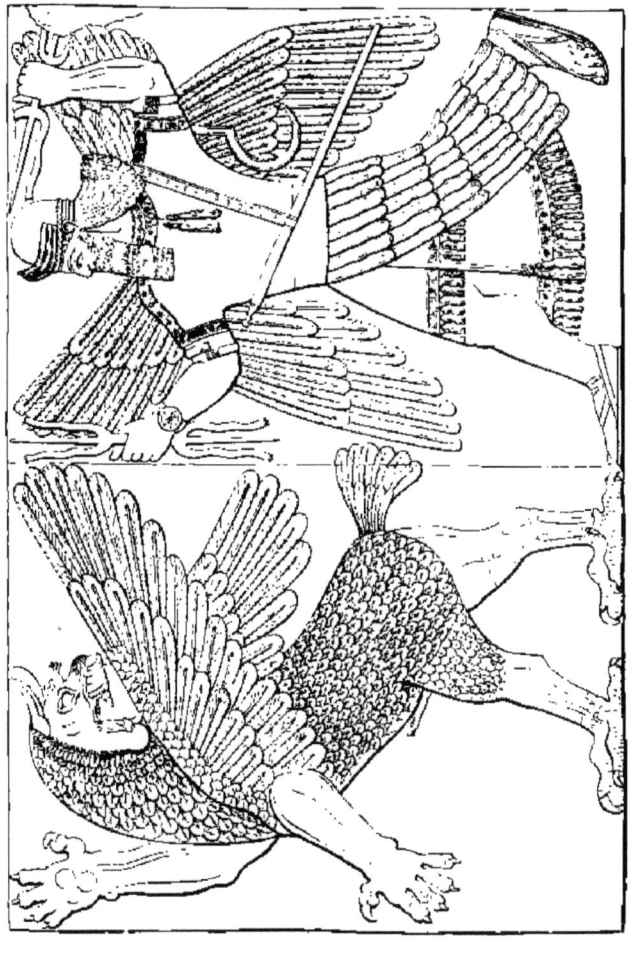

FIGHT BETWEEN MERODACH (BEL) AND THE DRAGON.

5. Those waters at the beginning were ordained; but

6. a tree had not grown, a flower had not unfolded.

7. When the gods had not sprung up, any one of them;

8. a plant had not grown, and order did not exist;

9. Were made also the great gods,

10. the gods Lahmu and Lahamu they caused to come . . . . .

11. and they grew . . . .

12. the gods Sar and Kisar were made . . . .

13. A course of days, and a long time passed . . .

14. the god Anu . . . . . .

15. the gods Sar and . . . . . .

16. . . . .

On the reverse of this tablet there are only fragments of the eight lines of colophon, but the restoration of the passage is easy, it reads :—

1. First tablet of "When above" (name of Creation series).

2. Palace of Assurbanipal king of nations, king of Assyria,

3. to whom Nebo and Tasmit attentive ears have given :

4. he sought with diligent eyes the wisdom of the inscribed tablets,

5. which among the kings who went before me,

6. none those writings had sought.

7. The wisdom of Nebo, the impressions? of the god my instructor? all delightful,

8. on tablets I wrote, I studied, I observed, and

9. for the inspection of my people within my palace I placed

This colophon will serve to show the value attached to the documents, and the date of the present copies.

The fragment of the obverse, broken as it is, is precious as giving the description of the chaos or desolate void before the Creation of the world, and the first movement of creation. This corresponds to the first two verses of the first chapter of Genesis.

1. "In the beginning God created the heaven and the earth.

2. And the earth was without form and void; and darkness was upon the face of the deep. And the spirit of God moved upon the face of the waters."

On comparing the fragment of the first tablet of the Creation with the extract from Damascius, we do not find any statement as to there being two principles at first called Tauthe and Apason, and these producing Moymis, but in the Creation tablet the first existence is called Mummu Tiamatu, a name meaning the "sea-water" or "sea chaos." The name Mummu Tiamatu combines the two names Moymis and Tauthe of Damascius. Tiamatu appears also as Tisallat and agrees with the Thalatth of Berosus, which we are expressly told was the sea. It is evident that, according to the notion of the Babylonians, the sea was the origin of all things, and this also agrees with the statement of Genesis, i. 2. where the chaotic waters are called םוהת, "the deep," the same word as the Tiamat of the Creation text and the Tauthe of Damascius.

The Assyrian word *Mummu* is probably connected with the Hebrew מהומה, confusion, and one of ·its equivalents is *Umun*, equal to the Hebrew המון noise or tumult. Beside the name of the chaotic deep called תהום in Genesis, which is, as I have said, evidently the Tiamat of the Creation text, we have in Genesis the word תהו, waste, desolate, or formless, applied to this chaos. This appears to be the tehuta of the Assyrians—a name of the sea-water (" History of Assurbanipal," p. 59); this word is closely connected with the word tiamat or tamtu, the sea. The correspondence between the inscription and Genesis is here complete, both stating that a watery chaos preceded the creation, and formed, in fact, the origin and groundwork of the universe. We have here not only an agreement in sense, but, what is rarer, the same word used in both narratives as the name of this chaos, and given also in the account of Damascius. Berosus has certainly the slightly different form Thalatth, with the same sense however, and it might be suspected that this word was a corruption of Tiamat, but the Babylonian word is read Tiamtu, Tiamat, and Tisallat, which last is more probably the origin of the word Thalatth of Berosus.

Next we have in the inscription the creation of the gods Lahma or Lahmu, and Lahama or Lahamu; these are male and female personifications of motion and production, and correspond to the Dache and

F

Dachus of Damascius, and the moving ᴔ, wind,
or spirit of Genesis. The next stage in the inscription gives the production of Sar or Ilsar, and Kisar,
representing the upper expanse and the lower expanse, and corresponding to the Assorus and Kissare
of Damascius. The resemblance in these names is
probably closer than here represented, for Sar or
Ilsar is generally read Assur as a deity in later times,
being an ordinary sign for the supreme god of the
Assyrians.

Here the cuneiform text becomes so mutilated
that little can be made out from it, but it appears
from the fragment of line 14 that the next step
was (as in Damascius) the generation of the three
great gods, Anu, Elu, and Hea, the Anus, Illinus,
and Aus of that writer. Anu represents the heaven,
Elu the earth, and Hea the sea, in this new form of
the universe.

It is probable that the inscription went on to
relate the generation of the other gods, and then
passed to the successive acts of creation by which
the world was fashioned.

The successive forms Lahma and Lahama, Sar and
Kisar, are represented in some of the god lists as
names or manifestations of Anu and Anatu. In each
case there appears to be a male and female principle,
which principles combine in the formation of the
universe.

The resemblance between the extract from Damascius and the account in the Creation tablet as to

these successive stages or forms in the Creation, is striking, and leaves no doubt that there was a connection between the two.

The three next tablets in the Creation series are absent, there being only two doubtful fragments of this part of the story. Judging from the analogy of the Book of Genesis, we may conjecture that this part of the narrative contained the description of the creation of light, of the atmosphere or firmament, of the dry land, and of plants. One fragment to which I have alluded as probably belonging to this space is a small portion of the top of a tablet referring to the fixing of the dry land; but it may belong to a later part of the story, for it is part of a speech to one of the gods. This fragment is—

1. When the foundations of the ground of rock [thou didst make]

2. the foundation of the ground thou didst call . .

3. thou didst beautify the heaven . . . . . .

4. to the face of the heaven . . . . . .

5. thou didst give . . . . . .

6. . . . . .

There is a second more doubtful fragment which appears to belong to this space, and, like the last, seems to relate part of the creation of the dry land. I give it here under reserve—

1. The god Sar . . . pan . . . . .

2. When to the god . . . .

3. Certainly I will cover? . . .

4. from the day that thou . . . .

5. angry thou didst speak . . . .

6. Sar (or Assur) his mouth opened · and spake, to the god . . . .

7. Above the sea which is the seat of . . . .

8. in front of the *esara* (firmament?) which I have made . . . .

9. below the place I strengthen it . . . .

10. Let there be made also *e-lu* (earth?) for the dwelling of [man?]

11. Within it his city may he build and . . . .

12. When from the sea he raised . . . .

13. the place . . . . lifted up . . . .

14. above . . . . heaven . . . .

15. the place . . . . lifted up . . . .

16. . . . . Pal-bi-ki the temples of the great gods . . . .

17. . . . . his father and his . . . . of him

18. the god . . . . thee and over all which thy hand has made

19. . . . . thee, having, over the earth which thy hand has made

20. . . . . having, Pal-bi-ki which thou hast called its name

21. . . . . made? my hand for ever

22. . . . . may they carry

23. the place . . . . any one the work which . . .

24. he rejoiced . . . . to after . . . .

25. the gods . . . . .

26. which in . . . . .

27. he opened . . . .

This fragment is both mutilated and obscure; in the eighth line I have translated firmament with a query, the sound and meaning of the word being doubtful; and in line 10, I translate earth for a combination of two characters more obscure still, my translation being a conjecture grounded on some meanings of the individual monograms. Pal-bi-ki are the characters of one name of the city of Assur; but I do not understand the introduction of this name here.

The next recognizable portion of the Creation legends is the upper part of the fifth tablet, which gives the creation of the heavenly bodies, and runs parallel to the account of the fourth day of creation in Genesis.

This tablet opens as follows:—

Fifth Tablet of Creation Legend.
Obverse.

1. It was delightful, all that was fixed by the great gods.

2. Stars, their appearance [in figures] of animals he arranged.

3. To fix the year through the observation of their constellations,

4. twelve months (or signs) of stars in three rows he arranged,

5. from the day when the year commences unto the close.

6. He marked the positions of the wandering stars (planets) to shine in their courses,

7. that they may not do injury, and may not trouble any one,

8. the positions of the gods Bel and Hea he fixed with him.

9. And he opened the great gates in the darkness shrouded

10. the fastenings were strong on the left and right.

11. In its mass (*i. e.* the lower chaos) he made a boiling,

12. the god Uru (the moon) he caused to rise out, the night he overshadowed,

13. to fix it also for the light of the night, until the shining of the day,

14. That the month might not be broken, and in its amount be regular.

15. At the beginning of the month, at the rising of the night,

16. his horns are breaking through to shine on the heaven.

17. On the seventh day to a circle he begins to swell,

18. and stretches towards the dawn further.

19. When the god Shamas (the sun) in the horizon of heaven, in the east,

20. . . . . formed beautifully and . . . .

21. . . . . . to the orbit Shamas was perfected

22. . . . . the dawn Shamas should change

23. . . . . going on its path

24. . . . . giving judgment
25. . . . . to tame
26. . . . . a second time
27. . . . .

Reverse.

1. . . . .
2. . . . . . he fixed

3. . . . of the gods on his hearing.

4. Fifth tablet of "When above" (Creation series).

5. Country of Assurbanipal king of nations king of Assyria.

This fine fragment is a typical specimen of the style of this series, and shows a marked stage in the Creation, the appointment of the heavenly orbs. It parallels the fourth day of Creation in the first chapter of Genesis, where we read : " And God said, Let there be lights in the firmament of the heaven to divide the day from the night ; and let them be for signs, and for seasons, and for days, and years :

" 15. And let them be for lights in the firmament of the heaven to give light upon the earth: and it was so.

" 16. And God made two great lights ; the greater light to rule the day, and the lesser light to rule the night ; he made the stars also.

" 17. And God set them in the firmament of the heaven to give light upon the earth,

" 18. And to rule over the day and over the night,

and to divide the light from the darkness: and God saw that it was good.

"19. And the evening and the morning were the fourth day."

The fragment of the first tablet of the Creation series showed that that was rather introductory, and dealt with the generation of the gods more than the creation of the universe, and the fact that the fifth tablet contains the Creation given in Genesis, under the fourth day, while a subsequent tablet, probably the seventh, gives the creation of the animals which, according to Genesis, took place on the sixth day, leads to the inference that the events of each of the days of Genesis were recorded on a separate tablet, and that the numbers of the tablets generally followed in the same order as the days of Creation in Genesis, thus:

Genesis, Chap. I.

V. 1 & 2 agree with Tablet 1.
V. 3 to 5 1st day   probably with tablet 2.
V. 6 to 8 2nd day probably with tablet 3.
V. 9 to 13 3rd day   probably with tablet 4.
V. 14 to 19 4th day   agree with tablet 5.
V. 20 to 23 5th day   probably with tablet 6.
V. 24 & 25 6th day   probably with tablet 7.

V. 26 and following, 6th and 7th day, probably with tablet 8.

The tablet which I think to be the eighth appears to give the Creation and Fall of Man, and is followed by several other tablets giving apparently the war between the gods and the powers of evil, but all of these are very mutilated, and no number can be positively proved beyond the fifth tablet. There is, however, fair reason to suppose that there was a close agreement in subjects and order between the text of the Chaldean legend and Genesis, while there does not appear to be anything like the same agreement between these inscriptions and the accounts trans-mitted to us through Berosus (see pp. 37-50).

The fifth tablet commences with the statement that the previous creations were "delightful," or satisfactory, agreeing with the oft-repeated statement of Genesis, after each act of creative power, that "God saw that it was good." The only difference here is one of detail. It appears that the Chaldean record contains the review and expression of satisfaction at the head of each tablet, while the Hebrew has it at the close of each act.

We then come to the creation of the heavenly orbs, which are described in the inscription as arranged like animals, while the Bible says they were set as "lights in the firmament of heaven," and just as the book of Genesis says they were set for signs and seasons, for days and years, so the inscription describes that the stars were set in courses to point out the year. The twelve constellations or signs of the zodiac, and two other bands of constellations are mentioned, just as two sets of twelve stars each are mentioned by the Greeks, one north and one south of the zodiac. I have translated one of these names

nibir, " wandering stars" or " planets," but this is not
the usual word for planet, and there is a star called
Nibir near the place where the sun crossed the
boundary between the old and new years, and this
star was one of twelve supposed to be favourable to
Babylonia.   It is evident, from the opening of the inscription on the first tablet of the Chaldean astrology
and astronomy, that the functions of the stars were
according to the Babylonians to act not only as regu-
lators of the seasons and the year, but to be also used
as signs, as in Genesis i. 14, for in those ages it was
generally believed that the heavenly bodies gave, by
their appearance and positions, signs of events which
were coming on the earth.

The passage given in the eighth line of the inscription, to the effect that the God who created the stars
fixed places or habitations for Bel and Hea with himself in the heavens, points to the fact that Anu, god
of the heavens, was considered to be the creator of
the heavenly hosts; for it is he who shares with Bel
and Hea the divisions of the face of the sky.

The ninth line of the tablet opens a curious view
as to the philosophical beliefs of the early Babylonians.   They evidently considered that the world
was drawn together out of the waters, and rested or
reposed upon a vast abyss of chaotic ocean which
filled the space below the world.   This dark infernal
lake was shut in by gigantic gates and strong fastenings, which prevented the floods from overwhelming
the world.   When the deity decided to create the

moon, he is represented as drawing aside the gates of this abyss, and creating a whirling motion like boiling in the dark ocean below; then, at his bidding, from this turmoil, arose the moon like a giant bubble, and, passing through the open gates, mounted on its destined way across the vaults of heaven.

The Babylonian account continues with the regulation of the motions of the moon to overshadow the night, to regulate and give light until the dawn of day. The phases of the moon are described: its commencing as a thin crescent at the evening on the first day of the month, and its gradually increasing and travelling further into the night. After the moon the creation of the sun is recorded, its beauty and perfection are extolled, and the regularity of its orbit, which led to its being considered the type of a judge, and the regulator of the world.

The Babylonian account of the Creation gives the creation of the moon before that of the sun, in reverse order to that in Genesis, and evidently the Babylonians considered the moon the principal body, while the Book of Genesis makes the sun the greater light. Here it is evident that Genesis is truer to nature than the Chaldean text.

The details of the creation of the planets and stars, which would have been very important to us, are unfortunately lost, no further fragment of this tablet having been recovered.

The colophon at the close of tablet V. gives us, however, part of the first line of the sixth tablet, but not enough to determine its subject. It is probable that this dealt with the creation of creatures of the water and fowls of the air, and that these were the creation of Bel, the companion deity to Anu.

The next tablet, the seventh in the series, is probably represented by a curious fragment, which I first found in one of the trenches at Kouyunjik, and recognized at once as a part of the description of the Creation.

This fragment is like some of the others, the upper portion of a tablet much broken, and only valuable from its generally clear meaning. The translation of this fragment is:

1. When the gods in their assembly had created . . . . .

2. were delightful the strong monsters . . . . .

3. they caused to be living creatures . . . . .

4. cattle of the field, beasts of the field, and creeping things of the field . . . . .

5. they fixed for the living creatures . . . . .

6. . . . . . cattle and creeping things of the city they fixed . . . . .

7. . . . . . the assembly of the creeping things the whole which were created . . . . .

8. . . . . . which in the assembly of my family . . . . .

9. . . . . . and the god Nin-si-ku (the lord of noble face) caused to be two . . . . .

10. . . . . . the assembly of the creeping things he caused to go . . . . .

11. . . . . . flesh beautiful? . . . . .
12. . . . . . pure presence . . . . .
13. . . . . . pure presence . . . . .

---

14. . . . . . pure presence in the assembly . . . .
15. . . . .

This tablet corresponds to the sixth day of Creation (Genesis, i. 24-25): "And God said, Let the earth bring forth the living creature after his kind, cattle, and creeping thing, and beast of the earth after his kind: and it was so.

"And God made the beast of the earth after his kind, and cattle after their kind, and everything that creepeth upon the earth after his kind: and God saw that it was good."

The Assyrian tablet commences with a statement of the satisfaction a former creation, apparently that of the monsters or whales, had given; here referring to Genesis i. 23. It then goes on to relate the creating of living animals on land, three kinds being distinguished, exactly agreeing with the Genesis account, and then we have in the ninth line a curious but broken account of Nin-si-ku (one of the names of Hea), creating two beings to be with the animals, the wording of the next fragmentary lines leading to the suspicion that this was the opening of the account of the creation of man. This, however, is only a suspicion, for the lines are so mutilated and obscure that nothing can be fairly proved from them. It is curious here, however, to notice a tablet which refers to the creation of man.   In this tablet, K 63, the creation of the human race is given to Hea, and all the references in other inscriptions make this his work.

In considering the next fragments, those which really relate to man, there is great difficulty; for, in the first fragment to be noticed, on one side the mutilation of the tablet renders the sense totally uncertain; in the space lost there may be a string of negatives which would entirely reverse the meaning. It is probable that the other side of the fragment is a discourse to the first woman on her duties. I think it to be the reverse of the tablet which, so far as it can be translated, appears to give the speech of the deity to the newly created pair (man and woman) instructing them in their duties.

K 3364 obverse.
(Many lines lost.)

1. evil . . . .
2. which is eaten by the stomach . . . .
3. in growing . . . .
4. consumed . . . .
5. extended, heavy, ...
6. firmly thou shalt speak . . . .
7. and the support of mankind . . . . thee
8. Every day thy god thou shalt approach (or invoke)
9. sacrifice, prayer of the mouth and instruments . . . . .
10. to thy god in reverence thou shalt carry.

11. Whatever shall be suitable for divinity,

12. supplication, humility, and bowing of the face,

13. fire? thou shalt give to him, and thou shalt bring tribute,

14. and in the fear also of god thou shalt be holy.

15. In thy knowledge and afterwards in the tablets (writing)

16. worship and goodness   shall be raised?

17. Sacrifice saving . . . .

18. and worship . . . .

19. the fear of god thou shalt not leave . . . .

20. the fear of the angels thou shalt live in . . . .

21. With friend and enemy? speech thou shalt make? . . . .

22. under? speech thou shalt make good . . . .

23. When thou shalt speak also he will give . . . .

24. When thou shalt trust also thou . . . .

25. to enemy? also . . . .

26. . . . . thou shalt trust a friend . . . .

27. . . . . thy knowledge also

Reverse.

(Many lines lost.)

1. Beautiful place also . . . . divide . . . .

2. in beauty and . . . . thy hand . . . .

3. and thou to the presence . . . . thou shalt fix . . . .

4. and not thy sentence . . . . thee to the end?

5. in the presence of beauty and . . . . thou shalt speak

6. of thy beauty and . . . .

7. beautiful and . . . . to give drink?

8. circle I fill? . . . . his enemies

9. his rising? he seeks . . . . the man . . . .

10. with the lord of thy beauty thou shalt be faithful,

11. to do evil thou shalt not approach him,

12. at thy illness . . . . to him

13. at thy distress . . . .

The obverse of this tablet is a fragment of the address from the deity to the newly created man on his duties to his god, and it is curious that while, in other parts of the story, various gods are mentioned by name, here only one god is mentioned, and simply as the "God." The fragments of this tablet might belong to the purest system of religion; but it would in this case be wrong to ground an argument on a single fragment.

The reverse of the tablet appears, so far as the sense can be ascertained, to be addressed to the woman, the companion of the man, informing her of her duties towards her partner.

The next fragment is a small one; it is the lower corner of a tablet with the ends of a few lines. It may possibly belong to the tablet of the Fall to be mentioned later.

. This fragment is of importance, small as it is, because it mentions a speech of Hea to man, and alludes to the Karkartiamat, or dragon of the sea, in connection with a revolt against the deity. The fragment is, however, too mutilated to give more than a general idea of its contents.

Obverse.

1. . . . . seat her
2. . . . . all the lords
3. . . . . his might
4. . . . . the gods, lord lofty?
5. . . . . kingdom exalted
6. . . . . in multitudes increase

Reverse.

1. . . . . Hea called to his man
2. . . . . height of his greatness
3. . . . . the rule of any god
4. . . . . Sartulku knew it
5. . . . . his noble . . . .
6. . . . . his fear? Sartulku
7. . . . . his might
8. . . . . to them, the dragon of the sea
9. . . . . against thy father fight

Connected with this fragment is the account of the curse after the Fall, on the remarkable fragment which I brought over from my first expedition to Assyria.

This forms about half a tablet, being part of the obverse and reverse, both in fair preservation; and so far as they go, fairly perfect, but containing at present many obscurities in the speeches of the gods. Before the commencement of lines 1, 5, 11, 19, 27, and 29 on the obverse, there are glosses stating that the divine titles commencing these lines all apply to the same deity. These explanatory glosses show that even in the Assyrian time there were difficulties in the narrative.

Obverse.

1. The god Zi . . . . .

2. which he had fixed . . . . .

3. their account . . . . .

4. may not fail in preparing ? . . . . .

5. The god Ziku (Noble life) quickly called; Director of purity,

6. good kinsman, master of perception and right,

7. causer to be fruitful and abundant, establisher of fertility,

8. another to us has come up, and greatly increased,

9. in thy powerful advance spread over him good,

10. may he speak, may he glorify, may he exalt his majesty.

11. The god Mir-ku (noble crown) in concern, raised a protection?

12. lord of noble lips, saviour from death

13. of the gods imprisoned, the accomplisher of restoration,

14. his pleasure he established he fixed upon the gods his enemies,

15. to fear them he made man,

16. the breath of life was in him.

17. May he be established, and may his will not fail,

18. in the mouth of the dark races which his hand has made.

19. The god of noble lips with his five fingers sin may he cut off;

20. who with his noble charms removes the evil curse.

21. The god Libzu wise among the gods, who had chosen his possession,

22. the doing of evil shall not come out of him,

23. established in the company of the gods, he rejoices their heart.

24. Subduer of the unbeliever . . . . .

25. director of right . . . . .

26. of corruption and . . . . .

27. The god Nissi . . . . .

28. keeper of watch . . . . .

29. The god Suhhab, swiftly . . . . .

30. the pourer out to them . . . . .

31. in . . . . .

32. like . . .

33. . . . . .

Reverse.

1. . . . . .

2. . . . . . the star . . . . .

3. may he take the tail and head . . . . .

4. because the dragon Tiamat had . . . . .

5. his punishment the planets possessing . . . .

6. by the stars of heaven themselves may they . .

7. like a sheep may the gods tremble all of them

8. may he bind Tiamat her prisons may he shut up and surround.

9. Afterwards the people of remote ages

10. may she remove, not destroy . . . for ever,

11. to the place he created, he made strong.

12. Lord of the earth his name called out, the father Elu

13. in the ranks of the angels pronounced their curse.

14. The god Hea heard and his liver was angry,

15. because his man had corrupted his purity.

16. He like me also Hea may he punish him,

17. the course of my issue all of them may he remove, and

18. all my seed may he destroy.

19. In the language of the fifty great gods

20. by his fifty names he called, and turned away in anger from him:

21. May he be conquered, and at once cut off.

22. Wisdom and knowledge hostilely may they injure him.

23. May they put at enmity also father and son and may they plunder.

24. to king, ruler, and governor, may they bend their ear.

25. May they cause anger also to the lord of the gods Merodach.

26. His land may it bring forth but he not touch it;

27. his desire shall be cut off, and his will be unanswered;

28. the opening of his mouth no god shall take notice of;

29. his back shall be broken and not be healed;

30. at his urgent trouble no god shall receive him;

31. his heart shall be poured out, and his mind shall be troubled;

32. to sin and wrong his face shall come . . . . .

33. . . . . front . . . . .

34. . . . .

In a second copy which presents several variations lines 14 to 19 are omitted.

This valuable fragment is unfortunately obscure in some parts, especially on the obverse, but the general meaning is undoubted, and the approximate position of the fragment in the story is quite clear. It evidently follows the fragment giving the creation of the land animals, and either forms a further portion of the same, or part of the following tablet.

The obverse gives a series of speeches and statements respecting the newly created man, who was supposed to be under the especial care of the deities. It happens in this case that there is no clue to the reason for these speeches, the key portions of the inscription being lost, but a point is evidently made of the purity of the man, who is said to be established in the company of the gods and to rejoice their hearts. The various divine titles or names, " the god of noble life," " the god of noble crown," and " the god of noble lips," are all most probably titles of Hea.

It appears from line 18 that the race of human beings spoken of is the *zalmat-qaqadi,* or dark race, and in various other fragments of these legends they are called Admi or Adami, which is exactly the name given to the first man in Genesis.

The word Adam used in these legends for the first human being is evidently not a proper name, but is only used as a term for mankind. Adam appears as a proper name in Genesis, but certainly in some passages is only used in the same sense as the Assyrian word, and we are told on the creation of human beings (Genesis, v. 1): "In the day that God created man, in the likeness of God made he him; male and female created he them; and blessed them, and called their name Adam, in the day when they were created."

It has already been pointed out by Sir Henry Rawlinson that the Babylonians recognized two principal races: the Adamu, or dark race, and the Sarku, or light race, probably in the same manner that two races are mentioned in Genesis, the sons of Adam and the sons of God. It appears incidentally from the fragments of inscriptions that it was the race of Adam, or the dark race, which was believed to have fallen, but there is at present no clue to the position of the other race in their system. We are informed in Genesis that when the world became corrupt the sons of God intermarried with the race of Adam, and thus spread the evils which had commenced with the Adamites (see Genesis, ch. vi.).

The obverse of the tablet giving the creation of man, where it breaks off leaves him in a state of purity, and where the narrative recommences on the reverse man has already fallen.

Here it is difficult to say how far the ·narrative of the inscription agrees with that of the Bible. In this case it is better to review the Biblical account, which is complete, and compare it with the fragmentary allusions in the inscriptions.

After the statement of man's innocence, which agrees with the inscription, the Bible goes on to relate (Genesis, iii. 1), that the serpent was more subtle than any beast of the field, and that he tempted the woman to sin. This attributes the origin of sin to the serpent, but nothing whatever is said as to the origin or history of the serpent. The fragmentary account of the Fall in the inscriptions mentions the dragon Tiamat, or the dragon of the sea, evidently in the same relation as the serpent, being concerned in bringing about the Fall. This dragon is called the dragon of tiamat or the sea; it is generally conceived of as a griffin, and is connected with the original chaos, the Thalatth of Berosus, the female principle which, according to both the inscriptions and Berosus, existed before the creation of the universe. This was the original spirit of chaos and disorder, a spirit opposed in principle to the gods, and, according to the Babylonians, self-existent and eternal, older even than the gods, for the birth or separation of the deities out of this chaos was the first step in the creation of the world.

According to Genesis, the serpent addressed the woman (Genesis, iii. 1), and inquired if God had forbidden them to eat of every tree of the Garden of

Eden, eliciting from her the statement that there was a tree in the middle of the Garden, the fruit of which was forbidden to them. There is nothing in the present fragments indicating a belief in the Garden of Eden or the Tree of Knowledge; there is only an obscure allusion in lines 16 and 22 to a thirst for knowledge having been a cause of man's fall, but outside these inscriptions, from the general body of Assyrian texts, Sir Henry Rawlinson has pointed out the agreement of the Babylonian region of Karduniyas or Ganduniyas with the Eden of the Bible. Eden is a fruitful place, watered by the four rivers, Euphrates, Tigris, Gihon, and Pison, and Ganduniyas is similar in description, watered by the four rivers, Euphrates, Tigris, Surappi, and Ukni. The loss of this portion of the Creation legend is unfortunate, as, however probable it may be that the Hebrew and Babylonian traditions agree about the Garden and Tree of Knowledge, we cannot now prove it. There is a second tree, the Tree of Life, in the Genesis account (ch. iii. 22), which certainly appears to correspond to the sacred grove of Anu, which a later fragment states was guarded by a sword turning to all the four points of the compass.

In several other places in the Genesis legends, and especially in the legends of Izdubar, there are allusions to the tree, grove, or forest of the gods, and this divine tree or grove is often represented on the sculptures, both in the Babylonian gem engravings, and on the walls of the Assyrian palaces and temples. When

the representation is complete, the tree is attended by
two figures of cherubims, one on each side of the sacred
emblem.

According to Genesis, Adam and Eve, tempted by

SACRED TREE, OR GROVE, WITH ATTENDANT CHERUBIM,
FROM ASSYRIAN CYLINDER.

the serpent, eat of the fruit of the Tree of Knowledge,
and so by disobedience brought sin into the world.
These details are also lost in the cuneiform text,
which opens again where the gods are cursing the
dragon and the Adam or man for this transgression,
corresponding to the passage, Genesis, iii. 9 to 19.
Throughout this, corresponding passages may be
found which show that the same idea runs through
both narratives, but some passages in the cuneiform
account are too mutilated to allow any certainty to
be attached to the translation, and the loss of the
previous parts of the text prevents our knowing
what points the allusions are directed to.

Although so much of the most important part of
the text is lost, the notices in other parts, and the
allusions in the mythological scenes on the Babylonian
gems will serve to guide us as to the probable drift
of the missing portion.

It is quite clear that the dragon of the sea or
dragon of Tiamat is connected with the Fall like the
serpent in the book of Genesis, and in fact is the
equivalent of the serpent.   The name of the dragon
is not written phonetically, but by two monograms
which probably mean the "scaly one," or animal
covered with scales. This description, of course,
might apply either to a fabulous dragon, a serpent,
or a fish.

The only passage where there is any phonetic explanation of the signs is in " Cuneiform Inscriptions,"
vol. ii. p. 32, l. 9, where we have *turbuhtu* for the
place or den of the dragon, perhaps connected with
the Hebrew תנים, sea-monster.   The form of this
creature as given on the gems is that of a griffin or
dragon generally with a head like a carnivorous animal,
body covered with scales, legs terminating in claws,
like an eagle, and wings on the back. Our own
heraldic griffins are so strikingly like the sculptures
of this creature that we might almost suspect them to
be copies from the Chaldean works.   In some cases,
however, the early Babylonian seals, which contained
devices taken from these legends, more closely approached the Genesis story.   One striking and important specimen of early type in the British Museum
collection has two figures sitting one on each side of a
tree, holding out their hands to the fruit, while at
the back of one is stretched a serpent. We know
well that in these early sculptures none of these
figures were chance devices, but all represented events

or supposed events, and figures in their legends; thus it is evident that a form of the story of the Fall, similar to that of Genesis, was known in early times in Babylonia.

The dragon which, in the Chaldean account of the

SACRED TREE, SEATED FIGURE ON EACH SIDE, AND SERPENT IN BACKGROUND, FROM AN EARLY BABYLONIAN CYLINDER.

Creation, leads man to sin, is the creature of Tiamat, the living principle of the sea and of chaos, and he is an embodiment of the spirit of chaos or disorder which was opposed to the deities at the creation of the world.

It is clear that the dragon is included in the curse for the Fall, and that the gods invoke on the head of the human race all the evils which afflict humanity. Wisdom and knowledge shall injure him (line 22), he shall have family quarrels (line 23), shall submit to tyranny (line 24), he will anger the gods (line 25), he shall not eat the fruit of his labour (line 26), he shall be disappointed in his desires (line 27), he shall pour out useless prayer (lines 28 and 30), he shall have trouble of mind and body (lines 29 and 31), he shall commit future sin (line 32). No doubt subsequent lines continue these topics, but again our narrative is broken, and it only reopens where the gods are preparing for war with the powers of evil, which are led by Tiamat, which war probably arose from the part played by Tiamat in the fall of man.

My first idea of this part was that the war with the powers of evil preceded the Creation; I now think it followed the account of the Fall, but I have no direct proof of this.

Of the subsequent tablets of this series, which include the war between the gods and powers of evil, and the punishment of the dragon Tiamat, there are several fragments.

The first of these is K 4832, too mutilated to translate, it contains speeches of the gods before the war.

The second fragment, K 3473, contains also speeches, and shows the gods preparing for battle. It is very fragmentary.

1. . . . . . his mouth opened
2. . . . . his . . a word he spoke
3. . . . . satisfy my anger
4. . . . . of thee let me send to thee
5. . . . . thou ascendest
6. . . . . thee to thy presence
7. . . . . their curse
8. . . . . in a circle may they sit
9. . . . . let them make the vine?
10. . . . . of them may they hear the renown
11. . . . . cover them he set and

12. . . . . thee change to them
13. . . . . he sent me
14. . . . . he held me
15. . . . . he sinned against me
16. . . . . and angrily . . . .
17. . . . . the gods all of them
18. . . . . made her hands . . . .
19. . . . . and his hand Tiamat coming
20. : . . . destroyed not night and day
21. . . . . burning . . .
22. . . . . they made division
23. . . . . the end of all hands
24. . . . . formerly thou . . . great serpents
25. . . . . unyielding I . . . .
26. . . . . their bodies fill . . . .
27. . . . . fear shall cover them
(Several other mutilated lines.)

The third fragment, K 3938, is on the same subject; some lines of this give the following general
meaning:—

1. great animal . . . .
2. fear he made to carry . . . .
3. their sight was very great . . . .
4. their bodies were powerful and . . . .
5. . . . . delightful, strong serpent . . . .
6. Udgallu, Urbat and . . . .
7. days arranged, five . . . . .
8. carrying weapons unyielding . . . .
9. her breast, her back . . . .
10. flowing? and first . . . .

11. among the gods collected . . . .

12. the god Kingu subdued . . . .

13. marching in front before . . . .

14. carrying weapons thou . . . .

15. upon war . . . .

16. his hand appointed

There are many more similar broken lines, and on the other side fragments of a speech by some being who desires Tiamat to make war.

All these fragments are not sufficiently complete to translate with certainty, or even to ascertain their order.

The fourth fragment, K 3449, relates to the making of weapons to arm the god who should meet in war the dragon.

This reads with some doubt on account of its mutilation:

1. heart . . . . .

2. burning . . . . .

3. from . . . . .

4. in the temple . . . . .

5. may he fix . . . . .

6. the dwelling of the god . . . . .

7. the great gods . . . . .

8. the gods said? . . . .

9. the sword that was made the gods saw

10. and they saw also the bow which was strung . . . . .

11. the work that was made they placed . . . . .

12. carried also Anu in the assembly of the gods . . . . .

13. the bow he fitted she . . . . .

14. and he spake of the bow thus and said

15. Noble wood who shall first thus draw thee? against ?

16. speed her punishment the star of the bow in heaven . . . . .

17. and establish the resting place of . . . . .

18. from the choice of . . . . .

19. and place his throne . . . . .

20. . . . . . in heaven . . . . .

21. . . . .

The next fragment or collection of fragments gives

BEL ENCOUNTERING THE DRAGON; FROM
BAYLONIAN CYLINDER.

the final struggle between Tiamat and Merodach or Bel, and this fragment appears to distinguish between the dragon of Tiamat or the sea monster, and Tiamat the female personification of the sea; but I am not sure of this distinction. The *saparu,* or sickle-shaped sword, is always represented both in the sculptures and inscriptions as a weapon of Bel in this war.

Sixth Fragment.

1. . . . . he fixed . . . .

2. . . . . to his right hand he distributed

3. . . . . and quiver his hand hurled,

4. the lightning he sent before him,

5. . . . . fierceness filled his body.

6. He made the sword to silence the dragon of the sea,

7. the seven winds he fixed not to come out of her wound.

8. On the South, the North, the East, and the West,

9. his hand the sword he caused to hold before the grove of his father the god Anu.

10. He made the evil wind, the hostile wind, the tempest, the storm,

11. the four winds, the seven winds, the wind of . . . ., the irregular wind.

12. He brought out the winds he had created seven of them,

13. the dragon of the sea stretched out, came after him,

14. he carried the thunderbolt his great weapon,

15. in a chariot . . . unrivalled, driving he rode:

16. he took her and four fetters on her hands he fastened,

17. . . . . : unyielding, storming . . . . her

18. . . . . with their sting bringing death

19. . . . . sweeping away knowledge

20. . . . . destruction and fighting

21. . . . . left hand . . . .

22. . . . . fear . . . .

(Several other fragmentary lines.)

Reverse.

1. . . . . . the god Sar . . . . .
2. . . . . . dwelling . . . . .
3. . . . . . before the weapon . . . . .
4. . . . . . field . . . . .
5. . . . . . above . . . . .
6. . . . . . struck to the god . . . . .
7. . . . . . them . . . . .
8. . . . . . cut into . . . . .
9. . . . . . said to his wife . . . . .
10. . . . . . him to break the god . . . . .
11. . . . . . evil? thou shalt be delivered and
12. . . . . . thy evil thou shalt subdue,
13. the tribute to thy maternity shall be forced upon them by thy weapons,
14. I will stand by and to thee they shall be made a spoil.
15. Tiamat on hearing this
16. at once joined and changed her resolution.
17. Tiamat called and quickly arose,
18. strongly and firmly she encircled with her defences,
19. she took a girdle? and placed . . . . .
20. and the gods for war prepared for them their weapons.
21. Tiamat attacked the just prince of the gods Merodach,
22. the standards they raised in the conflict like a battle.
23. Bel also drew out his sword and wounded her.

H

24. The evil wind coming afterwards struck against her face.

25. Tiamat opened her mouth to swallow him,

26. the evil wind he caused to enter, before she could shut her lips;

27. the force of the wind her stomach filled, and

28. her heart trembled, and her face was distorted,

29. . . . . . violently seized her stomach,

30. her inside it broke, and conquered her heart.

31. He imprisoned her, and her work he ended.

32. Her allies stood over her astonished,

33. when Tiamat their leader was conquered.

34. Her ranks he broke, her assembly was scattered,

35. and the gods her helpers who went beside her

36. trembled, feared, and broke up themselves,

37. the expiring of her life they fled from,

38. war surrounding they were fleeing not standing?

39. . . . . . them and their weapons he broke

40. like a sword cast down, sitting in darkness,

41. knowing their capture, full of grief,

42. their strength removed, shut in bonds,

43. and at once the strength of their work was overcome with terror,

44. the throwing of stones going . . . .

45. He cast down the enemy, his hand . . . .

46. part of the enemy under him . . . .

47. and the god Kingu again . . . .

48. . . . .

Again the main difficulty arises from the fragmentary state of the documents, it being impossible even to decide the order of the fragments. It appears, however, that the gods have fashioned for them a sword and a bow to fight the dragon Tiamat, and Anu proclaims great honour (fourth fragment, lines 15 to 20) to any of the gods who will engage in battle with her. Bel or Merodach volunteers, and goes forth armed with these weapons to fight the dragon. Tiamat is encouraged by one of the gods

MERODACH, OR BEL, ARMED FOR THE CONFLICT WITH THE DRAGON; FROM ASSYRIAN CYLINDER.

who has become her husband, and meets Merodach in battle. The description of the fight and the subsequent triumph of the god are very fine, and remarkably curious in their details, but the connection between the fragments is so uncertain at present that it is better to reserve comment upon them until the text is more complete. This war between the powers of good and evil, chaos and order, is extra to the Creation, does not correspond with anything in Genesis, but rather finds its parallel in the war

between Michael and the dragon in Revelation, xii.
7 to 9, where the dragon is called " the great dragon,
that old serpent, called the devil and Satan, which
deceiveth the whole world." This description is
strikingly like the impression gathered from the
fragments of the cuneiform story; the dragon Tiamat
who fought against the gods and led. man to sin, and
whose fate it was to be conquered in a celestial war,
closely corresponds in all essential points to the
dragon conquered by Michael. These fragments of
the cuneiform account of the Creation and Fall
agree so far as they are preserved with the Biblical
account, and show that in the period from B.C. 2000
to 1500 the Babylonians believed in a similar story
to that in Genesis.

FIGHT BETWEEN BEL AND THE DRAGON,
FROM BABYLONIAN CYLINDER.

Chapter VI.

OTHER BABYLONIAN ACCOUNTS OF THE CREATION.

Cuneiform accounts originally traditions. — Variations. — Account of Berosus. — Tablet from Cutha. — Translation. — Composite animals. — Eagle-headed men. — Seven brothers. — Destruction of men. — Seven wicked spirits. — War in heaven. — Variations of story. — Poetical account of Creation.

N the last chapter I have given the fragments of the principal story of the Creation and Fall from the cunei-form inscriptions, but it appears from the tablets that all these legends were "traditions" or "stories" repeated by word of mouth, and after-wards committed to writing. When such traditions are not reduced to writing, and depend on being handed down from generation to generation by word of mouth, they are liable to vary, sometimes very widely, according to the period and condition of the country. Thus many different versions of a story arise, and there can be no doubt that this was actually the case with the Creation legends. There must

have been a belief in the Creation and some of the leading features of this story long before these Creation legends were committed to writing, and there is evidence of other stories, related to those already given, which were at about the same time committed to writing. The story of the Creation transmitted through Berosus (see chapter iii. pp. 37-50) supplies us with a totally different story, differing entirely from the cuneiform account in the last chapter and from the Genesis account, and some fragments of tablets from Kouyunjik belonging to the library of Assurbanipal give a copy, mutilated as usual, of another version having many points of agreement with the account of Berosus. This legend, of which the following is a translation, is stated to be copied from a tablet at Cutha.

Legend of Creation from Cutha tablet.

(Many lines lost at commencement.)

1. lord of .*. . . .
2. . . . . his lord the strength of the gods . . . .
3. . . . . his host . . . . host . . . .
4. lord of the upper region and the lower region lord of angels . . . .
5. who drank turbid waters and pure water did not drink,
6. with his flame, his weapon, that man he enclosed,
7.   he took, he destroyed,
8. on a tablet nothing was then written, and there were not left the carcasses and waste?

EAGLE-HEADED MAN. FROM NIMROUD SCULPTURE.

9. from the earth nothing arose and I had not come to it.

10. Men with the bodies of birds of the desert, human beings

11. with the faces of ravens,

12. these the great gods created,

13. and in the earth the gods created for them a dwelling.

14. Tamat gave unto them strength,

15. their life the mistress of the gods raised,

16. in the midst of the earth they grew up and became great,

17. and increased in number,

18. Seven kings brothers of the same family,

19. six thousand in number were their people,

20. Banini their father was king, their mother

21. the queen was Milili,

22. their eldest brother who went before them, Mimangab was his name,

23. their second brother Midudu was his name,

24. their third brother . . . . tur was his name,

25. their fourth brother . . . . dada was his name,

26. their fifth brother . . . . tah was his name,

27. their sixth brother . . . . ru was his name,

28. their seventh brother . . . . was his name.

COLUMN II.

(Many lines lost.)

1. . . . . . . evil . . . .

2. man his will turned

3. in . . . . I purified?

4. On a tablet the evil curse of man he carved?

5. I called the worshippers and sent,

6. seven in width and seven in depth I arranged them.

7. I gave them noble reeds? (pipes?)

8. I worshipped also the great gods

·9. Ishtar, ... , Zamama, Anunitu

10. Nebo . . . . Shamas the warrior,

11. the gods listened to my doings

12. . . . . he did not give and

13. thus I said in my heart:

14. Now here am I and

15. let there not . . . . ground

16. let there not . . . .

17. may I go as I trust in Bel . . . . my heart,

18. and . . . . my iron may I take.

19. In the first year in the course of it

20. one hundred and twenty thousand men I sent out and among them,

21. one of them did not return.

22. In the second year in the course of it, ninety thousand the same.

23. In the third year in the course of it, sixty thousand seven hundred the same.

24. They were rooted out they were punished, I eat,

25. I rejoiced, I made a rest.

26. Thus I said in my heart now here am I and

27. at this time what is left?

28. I the king, am not the preserver of his country,

29. and the ruler is not the preserver of his people.

30. When I have done may corpses and waste be left,

31. the saving of the people from night, death, spirits, curses,

(Many more broken lines, meaning quite uncertain.)

FRAGMENT OF COLUMN III.

1. . . . I caused to pursue . . . .

2. . . . . blood . . . .

3. in the midst of them twelve men fled from me.

4. After them I pursued, swiftly I went,

5. those men, I captured them

6. those men I turned . . . . .

7. Thus I said in my heart . . . . . .

COLUMN IV.

(Several lines lost at commencement.)

1. to . . . . .

2. the powerful king . . . .

3. the gods . . . .

4. hand . . . . take them

5. thou king, viceroy, prince, or any one else,

6. whom God shall call, and who shall rule the kingdom,

7. who shall rebuild this house, this tablet I write to thee,

8. in the city of Cutha, in the temple of Sitlam,

9. in the sanctuary of Nergal, I leave for thee;

10. this tablet see, and,

11. to the words of this tablet listen, and

12. do not rebel, do not fail,

13. do not fear, and do not turn away,

14. then may thy support be established,

15. thou in thy works shall be glorious,

16. thy forts shall be strong,

17. thy canals shall be full of water,

18. thy treasures, thy corn, thy silver,

19. thy furniture, thy goods,

20. and thy instruments, shall be multiplied.

(A few more mutilated lines.)

SACRED TREE, ATTENDANT FIGURES AND EAGLE-HEADED MEN, FROM THE
SEAL OF A SYRIAN CHIEF, NINTH CENTURY B.C.

This is a very obscure inscription, the first column, however, forms part of a relation similar to that of Berosus in his history of the Creation; the beings who were killed by the light, and those with men's heads and bird's bodies, and bird's heads and men's bodies, agree with the composite monsters of Berosus, while the goddess of chaos, Tiamat, who is over them, is the same again as the Tiamat of the Creation legends and the Thalatth of Berosus.

The relation in the second and third columns of the inscription is difficult, and does not correspond with any known incident. The fourth column contains an address to any future king who should read the inscription which was deposited in the temple of Nergal at Cutha.

It is probable that this legend was supposed to be the work of one of the mythical kings of Chaldea, who describes the condition and history of the world before his time.

There is another legend which appears to be connected with these, the legend of the seven evil spirits, which I have given in my former work, "Assyrian Discoveries," p. 398.

Tablet with the story of the Seven Wicked Gods or Spirits.

Column I.

1. In the first days the evil gods
2. the angels who were in rebellion, who in the lower part of heaven
3. had been created,
4. they caused their evil work
5. devising with wicked heads . . .

6. ruling to the river . . . .

7. There were seven of them. The first was . . .

8. the second was a great animal . . . .

9.   which any one . . . .

10. the third was a leopard . . . .

11. the fourth was a serpent . . . .

12. the fifth was a terrible . . . . which to . . . .

13. the sixth was a striker which to god and king did not submit,

14. the seventh was the messenger of the evil wind which . . . . made.

15. The seven of them messengers of the god Anu their king

16. from city to city went round

17. the tempest of heaven was strongly bound to them,

18. the flying clouds of heaven surrounded them,

19. the downpour of the skies which in the bright day

20. makes darkness, was attached to them

21. with a violent wind, an evil wind, they began,

22. the tempest of Vul was their might,

23. at the right hand of Vul they came,

24. from the surface of heaven like lightning they darted,

25. descending to the abyss of waters, at first they came.

26. In the wide heavens of the god Anu the king

27. evil they set up, and an opponent they had not.

28. At this time Bel of this matter heard and

29. the account sank into his heart.

30. With Hea the noble sage of the gods he took counsel, and

31. Sin (the moon), Shamas (the sun), and Ishtar (Venus) in the lower part of heaven to control it he appointed.

32. With Anu to the government of the whole of heaven he set them up.

33. To the three of them the gods his children,

34. day and night to be united and not to break apart,

35. he urged them.

36. In those days those seven evil spirits

37. in the lower part of heaven commencing,

38. before the light of Sin fiercely they came,

39. the noble Shamas and Vul (the god of the atmosphere) the warrior to their side they turned and

40. Ishtar with Anu the king into a noble seat

41. they raised and in the government of heaven they fixed.

Column II.

1. The god . . . . .

2. . . . . . .

3. The god . . . . .

4. which . . . . .

5. In those days the seven of them . . . . .

6. at the head in the control to . . . . .

7. evil . . . . .

8. for the drinking of his noble mouth . . . .

9. The god Sin the ruler . . . . mankind

10. . . . . . of the earth

11. . . . . . troubled and on high he sat,

12. night and day fearing, in the seat of his dominion he did not sit.

13. Those evil gods the messengers of Anu their king

14. devised with wicked heads to assist one another, and

15. evil they spake together, and

16. from the midst of heaven like a wind to the earth they came down.

17. The god Bel of the noble Sin, his trouble

18. in heaven, he saw and

19. Bel to his attendant the god Nusku said:

20. " Attendant Nusku this account to the ocean carry, and

21. the news of my child Sin who in heaven is greatly troubled;

22. to the god Hea in the ocean repeat."

23. Nusku the will of his lord obeyed, and

24. to Hea in the ocean descended and went.

25. To the prince, the noble sage, the lord, the god unfailing,

26. Nusku the message of his lord at once repeated.

27. Hea in the ocean that message heard, and

28. his lips spake, and with wisdom his mouth was filled.

29. Hea his son the god Merodach called, and this word he spake:

30. " Go my son Merodach

31. enter into the shining Sin who in heaven is greatly troubled;

32. his trouble from heaven expel.

33. Seven of them the evil gods, spirits of death, having no fear,

34. seven of them the evil gods, who like a flood

35. descend and sweep over the earth.

36. To the earth like a storm they come down.

37. Before the light of Sin fiercely they came

38. the noble Shamas and Vul the warrior, to their side they turned and . . . .

The end of this legend is lost; it probably recorded the interference of Merodach in favour of Sin, the moon god.

In this story, which differs again from all the others, Bel is supposed to place in the heaven the Moon, Sun, and Venus, the representative of the stars. The details have no analogy with the other stories, and this can only be considered a poetical myth of the Creation.

This legend is part of the sixteenth tablet of the series on evil spirits; but the tablet contains other matters as well, the legend apparently being only quoted in it. There is another remarkable legend of the same sort on another tablet of this series

Ingram Content Group UK Ltd.
Milton Keynes UK
UKHW011603060323
418105UK00009B/1126